ESCAPE FROM CAMP 14

ESCAPE FROM CAMP 14

ONE MAN'S REMARKABLE ODYSSEY FROM NORTH KOREA TO FREEDOM IN THE WEST

BLAINE HARDEN

VIKING

VIKING
Published by the Penguin Group
Penguin Group (USA) Inc., 375 Hudson Street, New York, New York 10014, U.S.A. • Penguin Group (Canada), 90 Eglinton Avenue East, Suite 700, Toronto, Ontario, Canada M4P 2Y3 • (a division of Pearson Penguin Canada Inc.) • Penguin Books Ltd, 80 Strand, London WC2R 0RL, England • Penguin Ireland, 25 St. Stephen's Green, Dublin 2, Ireland (a division of Penguin Books Ltd) • Penguin Books Australia Ltd, 250 Camberwell Road, Camberwell, Victoria 3124, Australia • (a division of Pearson Australia Group Pty Ltd) • Penguin Books India Pvt Ltd, 11 Community Centre, Panchsheel Park, New Delhi – 110 017, India • Penguin Group (NZ), 67 Apollo Drive, Rosedale, Auckland 0632, New Zealand (a division of Pearson New Zealand Ltd) • Penguin Books (South Africa) (Pty) Ltd, 24 Sturdee Avenue, Rosebank, Johannesburg 2196, South Africa

Penguin Books Ltd, Registered Offices:
80 Strand, London WC2R 0RL, England

First published in 2012 by Viking Penguin,
a member of Penguin Group (USA) Inc.

10   9   8

Photograph and drawing credits
Insert page 1 (top), 2 (bottom) (photo of government image), 3 (top and bottom) (photos of paintings), 6 (top), 7 (top), 8: Photos by Blaine Harden
1 (bottom): Kyodo via AP Images
2 (top): Korean Central News Agency / Korea News Service via AP Images
4 and 5 (six drawings): From *Escape to the Outside World* by Shin Dong-hyuk, courtesy of the publisher, Database Center for North Korean Human Rights
6 (bottom): Jennifer Cho
7 (bottom): Courtesy of Lowell and Linda Dye

LIBRARY OF CONGRESS CATALOGING IN PUBLICATION DATA
Harden, Blaine.
Escape from Camp 14 : one man's remarkable odyssey from North Korea to freedom in the West / Blaine Harden.
   p.   cm.
Includes bibliographical references.
ISBN 978-0-670-02332-5
1. Shin, Dong-hyuk. 2. Political prisoners—Korea (North)—Biography. 3. Concentration camps—Korea (North) 4. Forced labor—Korea (North) 5. Korea (North)—Social conditions. I. Title.
HV9815.6.H37 2012
365'.45092—dc23
[B]
2011037555

Printed in the United States of America
Set in Warnock Pro with Foundry Gridnik
Designed by Daniel Lagin
Maps by Jeffrey L. Ward

For North Koreans who remain in the camps

There is no "human rights issue" in this country, as everyone leads the most dignified and happy life.

—[North] Korean Central News Agency, March 6, 2009

SHIN'S MAP OF CAMP 14

1 Shin Dong-hyuk's home
2 Execution grounds
3 Shin's school
4 Shin's class harassed by guards' children
5 Dam where Shin worked and retrieved bodies
6 Pig farm where Shin worked
7 Textile plant where Shin learned about the outside world
8 Fence line where Shin escaped

Taedong River

0 Miles 2 4
0 Kilometers 4

NORTH KOREA

130°
RUSSIA
125°

0 Miles 100 200
0 Kilometers 200

CHINA

CAMP 14

Sea of
Japan

40°

40°

Korea
Bay

★ Pyongyang

Yellow
Sea

125°

SOUTH
KOREA

130°

KEY

— Camp fence
⊚ Guard Post
1 Shin Dong-hyuk's home
2 Execution grounds
3 Shin's school
4 Shin's class harassed by guards' children
5 Dam where Shin worked and retrieved bodies
6 Pig farm where Shin worked
7 Textile plant where Shin learned about the outside world
8 Fence line where Shin escaped

© 2012 Jeffrey L. Ward

PREFACE

A TEACHABLE MOMENT

His first memory is an execution.

He walked with his mother to a wheat field near the Taedong River, where guards had rounded up several thousand prisoners. Excited by the crowd, the boy crawled between adult legs to the front row, where he saw guards tying a man to a wooden pole.

Shin In Geun was four years old, too young to understand the speech that came before that killing. At dozens of executions in years to come, he would listen to a supervising guard telling the crowd that the prisoner about to die had been offered "redemption" through hard labor, but had rejected the generosity of the North Korean government. To prevent the prisoner from cursing the state that was about to take his life, guards stuffed pebbles into his mouth, then covered his head with a hood.

At that first execution, Shin watched three guards take aim. Each fired three times. The reports of their rifles terrified the boy and he fell over backward. But he scrambled to his feet in time to see guards untie a slack, blood-spattered body, wrap it in a blanket, and heave it into a cart.

In Camp 14, a prison for the political enemies of North Korea, assemblies of more than two inmates were forbidden, except for executions. Everyone had to attend them. The labor camp used a public killing—and the fear it generated—as a teachable moment.

Shin's guards in the camp were his teachers—and his breeders. They had selected his mother and father. They taught him that prisoners who break camp rules deserve death. On a hillside near his school, a slogan was posted: ALL ACCORDING TO THE RULES AND REGULATIONS. The boy memorized the camp's ten rules, "The Ten Commandments," as he later called them, and can still recite them by heart. The first one stated: "Anyone caught escaping will be shot immediately."

Ten years after that first execution, Shin returned to the same field. Again, guards had rounded up a big crowd. Again, a wooden pole had been pounded in the ground. A makeshift gallows had also been built.

Shin arrived this time in the backseat of a car driven by a guard. He wore handcuffs and a blindfold fashioned from a rag. His father, also handcuffed and blindfolded, sat beside him in the car.

They had been released from eight months in an underground prison inside Camp 14. As a condition of their release, they had signed documents promising never to discuss what had happened to them underground.

In that prison within a prison, guards tried to torture a confession out of Shin and his father. They wanted to know about the failed escape of Shin's mother and only brother. Guards stripped Shin, tied ropes to his ankles and wrists, and suspended him from a hook in the ceiling. They lowered him over a fire. He passed out when his flesh began to burn.

But he confessed nothing. He had nothing to confess. He had not conspired with his mother and brother to escape. He believed what guards had taught him since his birth inside the camp: He could never escape and he must inform on anyone who talks about trying. Not even in his dreams had Shin fantasized about life on the outside.

Guards never taught him what every North Korean schoolboy learns: Americans are "bastards" scheming to invade and humiliate the homeland. South Korea is the "bitch" of its American master. North Korea is a great country whose brave and brilliant leaders are the envy of the world. Indeed, he knew nothing of the existence of South Korea, China, or the United States.

Unlike his countrymen, he did not grow up with the ubiquitous photograph of his Dear Leader, as Kim Jong Il was called. Nor had he seen photographs or statues of Kim's father, Kim Il Sung, the Great Leader who founded North Korea and who remains the country's Eternal President, despite his death in 1994.

Although he had not been important enough for brainwashing, Shin had been schooled to inform on his family and on his classmates. He won food as a reward and joined guards in beating up children he betrayed. His classmates, in turn, tattled on him and beat him up.

When a guard removed his blindfold, when he saw the crowd, the wooden pole, and the gallows, Shin believed he was about to be executed.

No pebbles, though, were forced into his mouth. His handcuffs were removed. A guard led him to the front of the crowd. He and his father would be spectators.

Guards dragged a middle-aged woman to the gallows and tied a young man to the wooden pole. They were Shin's mother and his older brother.

A guard tightened a noose around his mother's neck. She tried to catch his eye. He looked away. After she stopped twitching at the end of the rope, Shin's brother was shot by three guards. Each fired three times.

As he watched them die, Shin was relieved it was not him. He was angry with his mother and brother for planning an escape. Although he would not admit it to anyone for fifteen years, he knew he was responsible for their executions.

ESCAPE FROM CAMP 14

INTRODUCTION

NEVER HEARD
THE WORD "LOVE"

Nine years after his mother's hanging, Shin squirmed through an electric fence and ran off through the snow. It was January 2, 2005. Before then, no one born in a North Korean political prison camp had ever escaped. As far as can be determined, Shin is still the only one to do it.

He was twenty-three years old and knew no one outside the fence.

Within a month, he had walked into China. Within two years, he was living in South Korea. Four years later, he was living in Southern California and was a senior ambassador at Liberty in North Korea (LiNK), an American human rights group.

In California, he rode his bike to work, followed the Cleveland Indians (because of their South Korean slugger, Shin-Soo Choo), and ate two or three times a week at In-N-Out Burger, which he viewed as the world's finest burger.

His name is now Shin Dong-hyuk.* He changed it after arriving in South Korea, an attempt to reinvent himself as a free man. He is handsome, with quick, wary eyes. A Los Angeles dentist has done work on

---

* North Korean names are not hyphenated; South Korean names are.

his teeth, which he could not brush in the camp. His overall physical health is excellent. His body, though, is a road map of the hardships of growing up in a labor camp that the North Korean government insists does not exist.

Stunted by malnutrition, he is short and slight—five feet six inches, about one hundred and twenty pounds. His arms are bowed from childhood labor. His lower back and buttocks are scarred with burns from the torturer's fire. The skin over his pubis bears a puncture scar from the hook used to hold him in place over the fire. His ankles are scarred by shackles, from which he was hung upside down in solitary confinement. His right middle finger is cut off at the first knuckle, a guard's punishment for dropping a sewing machine in a camp garment factory. His shins, from ankle to knee on both legs, are mutilated and scarred by burns from the electrified barbed-wire fence that failed to keep him inside Camp 14.

Shin is roughly the same age as Kim Jong Eun, the chubby third son of Kim Jong Il who took over as leader after his father's death in 2011. As contemporaries, Shin and Kim Jong Eun personify the antipodes of privilege and privation in North Korea, a nominally classless society where, in fact, breeding and bloodlines decide everything.

Kim Jong Eun was born a communist prince and raised behind palace walls. He was educated under an assumed name in Switzerland and returned to North Korea to study in an elite university named after his grandfather. Because of his parentage, he lives above the law. For him, everything is possible. In 2010, he was named a four-star general in the Korean People's Army despite a total lack of field experience in the military. A year later, after his father died of a sudden heart attack, state media in North Korea described him as "another leader sent from heaven." He may, however, be forced to share his earthly dictatorship with relatives and military leaders.

Shin was born a slave and raised behind a high-voltage barbed-wire fence. He was educated in a camp school to read and count at a rudimentary level. Because his blood was tainted by the perceived crimes of his father's brothers, he lived below the law. For him, nothing was possible. His state-prescribed career trajectory was hard labor and an early death from disease brought on by chronic hunger—all without a charge or a trial or an appeal, and all in secrecy.

In stories of concentration camp survival, there is a conventional narrative arc. Security forces steal the protagonist away from a loving family and a comfortable home. To survive, he abandons moral principles, suppresses feelings for others, and ceases to be a civilized human being.

In perhaps the most celebrated of these stories, *Night*, by Nobel Prize winner Elie Wiesel, the thirteen-year-old narrator explains his torment with an account of the normal life that existed before he and his family were packed aboard trains bound for Nazi death camps. Wiesel studied the Talmud daily. His father owned a store and watched over their village in Romania. His grandfather was always present to celebrate the Jewish holidays. But after the boy's entire family perished in the camps, Wiesel was left "alone, terribly alone in a world without God, without man. Without love or mercy."

Shin's story of survival is different.

His mother beat him, and he viewed her as a competitor for food. His father, who was allowed by guards to sleep with his mother just five nights a year, ignored him. His brother was a stranger. Children in the camp were untrustworthy and abusive. Before he learned anything else, Shin learned to survive by snitching on all of them.

Love and mercy and family were words without meaning. God did not disappear or die. Shin had never heard of him.

In a preface to *Night*, Wiesel wrote that an adolescent's knowledge of death and evil "should be limited to what one discovers in literature."

In Camp 14, Shin did not know literature existed. He saw only one book in the camp, a Korean grammar, in the hands of a teacher who wore a guard's uniform, carried a revolver on his hip, and beat one of his primary school classmates to death with a chalkboard pointer.

Unlike those who have survived a concentration camp, Shin had not been torn away from a civilized existence and forced to descend into hell. He was born and raised there. He accepted its values. He called it home.

North Korea's labor camps have now existed twice as long as the Soviet Gulag and about twelve times longer than the Nazi concentration camps. There is no dispute about where these camps are. High-resolution satellite photographs, accessible on Google Earth to anyone with an Internet connection, show vast fenced compounds sprawling through the rugged mountains of North Korea.

The South Korean government estimates there are about one hundred fifty-four thousand prisoners in the camps, while the U.S. State Department and several human rights groups have put the number as high as two hundred thousand. After examining a decade of satellite images of the camps, Amnesty International noticed new construction inside the camps in 2011 and became concerned that the inmate population was increasing, perhaps to short-circuit possible unrest as power began to shift from Kim Jong Il to his young and untried son.[1]

There are six camps, according to South Korea's intelligence agency and human rights groups. The biggest is thirty-one miles long and twenty-five miles wide, an area larger than the city of Los Angeles. Electrified barbed-wire fences—punctuated by guard towers and patrolled by armed men—encircle most of the camps. Two of them, numbers 15 and 18, have reeducation zones where some fortunate detainees receive remedial instruction in the teachings of Kim Jong Il and Kim Il Sung. If prisoners memorize enough of these teachings and convince guards they are loyal, they can be released, but they are monitored for the rest of their lives by state security.

The remaining camps are "complete control districts" where prisoners, who are called "irredeemables,"[2] are worked to death.

Shin's camp, number 14, is a complete control district. By reputation it is the toughest of them all because of its particularly brutal working conditions, the vigilance of its guards, and the state's unforgiving view of the seriousness of the crimes committed by its inmates, many of whom are purged officials from the ruling party, the government, and the military, along with their families. Established in 1959 in central North Korea—Kaechon, South Pyongan Province—Camp 14 holds an estimated fifteen thousand prisoners. About thirty miles long and fifteen miles wide, it has farms, mines, and factories threaded through steep mountain valleys.

Although Shin is the only one born in a labor camp to escape to tell his story, there are at least twenty-six other eyewitnesses from the labor camps now in the free world.[3] They include at least fifteen North Koreans who were imprisoned in Camp 15's edification district, won their release, and later turned up in South Korea. Former guards from other camps have also found their way to South Korea. Kim Yong, a former North Korean lieutenant colonel from a privileged background in Pyongyang, spent six years in two camps before escaping in a coal train.

A distillation of their testimony by the Korean Bar Association in Seoul paints a detailed picture of daily life in the camps. A few prisoners are publicly executed every year. Others are beaten to death or secretly murdered by guards, who have almost complete license to abuse and rape prisoners. Most prisoners tend crops, mine coal, sew military uniforms, or make cement while subsisting on a near-starvation diet of corn, cabbage, and salt. They lose their teeth, their gums turn black, their bones weaken, and, as they enter their forties, they hunch over at the waist. Issued a set of clothes once or twice a year, they commonly work and sleep in filthy rags, living without soap, socks, gloves, underclothes, or toilet paper. Twelve- to fifteen-hour workdays are mandatory until prisoners die, usually of malnutrition-related illnesses, before they turn fifty.[4] Although precise numbers are impossible to obtain, Western governments and human rights groups estimate that hundreds of thousands of people have perished in these camps.

Most North Koreans are sent to the camps without any judicial process, and many die there without learning the charges against them. They are taken from their homes, usually at night, by the Bowibu, the National Security Agency. Guilt by association is legal in North Korea. A wrongdoer is often imprisoned with his parents and children. Kim Il Sung laid down the law in 1972: "[E]nemies of class, whoever they are, their seed must be eliminated through three generations."

My first encounter with Shin was at lunch in the winter of 2008. We met in a Korean restaurant in downtown Seoul. Talkative and hungry, he wolfed down several helpings of rice and beef. As he ate, he told my translator and me what it was like to watch as his mother was hanged. He blamed her for his torture in the camp, and he went out of his way to say that he was still furious with her. He said he had not been a "good son," but would not explain why.

During his years in the camp he said he had never once heard the word "love," certainly not from his mother, a woman he continued to despise, even in death. He had heard about the concept of forgiveness in a South Korean church. But it confused him. To ask for forgiveness in Camp 14, he said, was "to beg not to be punished."

He had written a memoir about the camp, but it had received little attention in South Korea. He was jobless, broke, behind on his rent, and uncertain what to do next. The rules of Camp 14 had prevented him, on pain of execution, from having intimate contact with a woman. He now wanted to find a proper girlfriend, but said he didn't know how to begin looking for one.

After lunch, he took me to the small, sad apartment in Seoul that he could not afford. Although he would not look me in the eye, he showed me his chopped-off finger and his scarred back. He allowed me to take his photograph. For all the hardship he had endured he had a baby face. He was twenty-six years old—three years out of Camp 14.

I was fifty-six years old at that memorable lunch. As a correspondent for the *Washington Post* in Northeast Asia, I had been searching for more than a year for a story that could explain how North Korea used repression to keep from falling apart.

Political implosion had become my specialty. For the *Post* and for the *New York Times*, I spent nearly three decades covering failed states in Africa, the collapse of communism in Eastern Europe, the breakup of Yugoslavia, and the slow-motion rot in Burma under the generals. From the outside looking in, North Korea seemed ripe—indeed, overripe—for the kind of collapse I had witnessed elsewhere. In a part of the world where nearly everyone else was getting rich, its people were increasingly isolated, poor, and hungry.

Still, the Kim family dynasty kept the lid on. Totalitarian repression preserved their basket case state.

My problem in showing how the government did it was lack of access. Elsewhere in the world, repressive states were not always successful in sealing their borders. I had been able to work openly in Mengistu's Ethiopia, Mobutu's Congo, and Milosevic's Serbia, and had slipped in as a tourist to write about Burma.

North Korea was much more careful. Foreign reporters, especially Americans, were rarely allowed inside. I visited North Korea only once, saw what my minders wanted me to see, and learned little. If journalists entered illegally, they risked months or years of imprisonment as spies. To win release, they sometimes needed the help of a former American president.[5]

Given these restrictions, most reporting about North Korea was distant and hollow. Written from Seoul or Tokyo or Beijing, stories began with an account of Pyongyang's latest provocation, such as sinking a ship or shooting a tourist. Then the dreary conventions of journalism kicked in: American and South Korean officials expressed outrage. Chinese officials called for restraint. Think tank experts opined about what it might mean. I wrote more than my share of these pieces.

Shin, though, shattered these conventions. His life unlocked the door, allowing outsiders to see how the Kim family sustained itself with child slavery and murder. A few days after we met, Shin's appealing picture and appalling story ran prominently on the front page of the *Washington Post*.

"Wow," wrote Donald G. Graham, chairman of the Washington Post Company, in a one-word e-mail I received the morning after the story appeared. A German filmmaker, who happened to be visiting Washington's Holocaust Memorial Museum on the day the story was published, decided to make a documentary about Shin's life. The *Washington Post* ran an editorial saying that the brutality Shin endured was horrifying, but just as horrifying was the world's indifference to the existence of North Korea's labor camps.

"High school students in America debate why President Franklin D. Roosevelt didn't bomb the rail lines to Hitler's camps," the editorial concluded. "Their children may ask, a generation from now, why the West stared at far clearer satellite images of Kim Jong Il's camps, and did nothing."

Shin's story seemed to get under the skin of ordinary readers. They wrote letters and sent e-mails, offering money, housing, and prayers.

A married couple in Columbus, Ohio, saw the article, located Shin, and paid for him to travel to the United States. Lowell and Linda Dye told Shin they wanted to be the parents he never had.

A young Korean American woman in Seattle, Harim Lee, read the story and prayed that she would meet Shin. She later sought him out in Southern California and they fell in love.

My article had only skimmed the surface of Shin's life. It struck me that a deeper account would unveil the secret machinery that enforces totalitarian rule in North Korea. It would also show—through the details of Shin's improbable flight—how some of that oppressive machinery is breaking down, allowing an unworldly young escapee to wander undetected across a police state and cross into China. As important, no one who read a book about a boy bred by North Korea to be worked to death could ever ignore the existence of the camps.

I asked Shin if he was interested. It took him nine months to make up his mind. During those months, human rights activists in South Korea, Japan, and the United States urged him to cooperate, telling him that a book in English would raise world awareness, increase international pressure on North Korea, and perhaps put some much needed money in his pocket. After Shin said yes, he made himself available for seven rounds of interviews, first in Seoul, then in Torrance, California, and finally in Seattle, Washington. Shin and I agreed to a fifty-fifty split of whatever it might earn. Our agreement, though, gave me control over the contents.

Shin began keeping a diary in early 2006, about a year after his escape from North Korea. In Seoul, after he was hospitalized for depression, he continued writing in it. The diary became the basis for his Korean-language memoir, *Escape to the Outside World*, which was published in Seoul in 2007 by the Database Center for North Korean Human Rights.

The memoir was a starting point for our interviews. It was also the source for many of the direct quotations that are attributed in this book to Shin, his family, friends, and prison keepers during the time he was in North Korea and China. But every thought and action attributed to Shin in these pages is based on multiple interviews with him, during which he expanded upon and, in many crucial instances, corrected his Korean memoir.

Even as he cooperated, Shin seemed to dread talking to me. I often felt like a dentist drilling without anesthetics. The drilling went on intermittently for more than two years. Some of our sessions were cathartic for him; many others made him depressed.

He struggled to trust me. As he readily admits, he struggles to trust anyone. It is an inescapable part of how he was raised. Guards taught him to sell out his parents and friends, and he assumes everyone he meets will sell him out in turn.

In writing this book, I have sometimes struggled to trust him. He misled me in our first interview about his role in the death of his mother, and he continued to do so in more than a dozen interviews. When he changed his story, I became worried about what else he might have made up.

Fact-checking is not possible in North Korea. Outsiders have not visited its political prison camps. Accounts of what goes on inside them cannot be independently verified. Although satellite images have greatly added to outside understanding of the camps, defectors remain the primary sources of information, and their motives and credibility are not spotless. In South Korea and elsewhere, they are often desperate to make a living, willing to confirm the preconceptions of human rights activists, anticommunist missionaries, and right-wing ideologues. Some camp survivors refuse to talk unless they are paid cash upfront. Others repeated juicy anecdotes they had heard but not personally witnessed.

While Shin remained wary of me, he responded to every question about his past that I could think of. His life can seem incredible, but it echoes the experiences of other former prisoners in the camps, as well as the accounts of former camp guards.

"Everything Shin has said is consistent with what I have heard about the camps," said David Hawk, a human rights specialist who has interviewed Shin and more than two dozen other former labor camp prisoners for "The Hidden Gulag: Exposing North Korea's Prison Camps," a report that links survivor accounts with annotated satellite images. It was first published in 2003 by the U.S. Committee for Human Rights in North Korea and has been updated as more testimony and higher-resolution satellite images became available. Hawk told me that because Shin was born and raised in a camp, he knows things that other camp survivors do not. Shin's story has also been vetted by the authors of the Korean Bar Association's "White Paper on Human Rights in North Korea 2008." They conducted extensive interviews with Shin, as well as with other known camp survivors willing to talk. As Hawk has written, the only way for North Korea to "refute, contradict, or invalidate" the testimony of Shin and other camp survivors would be to permit outside experts to visit the camps. Otherwise, Hawk declares, their testimony stands.

If North Korea does collapse, Shin may be correct in predicting that its leaders, fearing war crimes trials, will demolish the camps before investigators can get to them. As Kim Jong Il explained, "We must envelope our environment in a dense fog to prevent our enemies from learning anything about us."[6]

To try to piece together what I could not see, I spent the better part of three years reporting about North Korea's military, leadership, economy, food shortages, and human rights abuses. I interviewed scores of North Korean defectors, including three former inmates of Camp 15 and a former camp guard and driver who worked at four labor camps. I spoke to South Korean scholars and technocrats who travel regularly inside North Korea, and I reviewed the growing body of scholarly research on and personal memoirs about the camps. In the United States, I conducted extended interviews with Korean Americans who have become Shin's closest friends.

In assessing Shin's story, one should keep in mind that many others in the camps have endured similar or worse hardships, according to An Myeong Chul, a former camp guard and driver. "Shin had a relatively comfortable life by the standards of other children in the camps," An said.

By exploding nuclear bombs, attacking South Korea, and cultivating a reputation for hair-trigger belligerence, the government of North Korea has stirred up a semipermanent security emergency on the Korean Peninsula.

When North Korea deigns to enter into international diplomacy, it has always succeeded in shoving human rights off any negotiating table. Crisis management, usually focused on nuclear weapons and missiles, has dominated American dealings with the North.

The labor camps have been an afterthought.

"Talking to them about the camps is something that has not been possible," David Straub, who worked in the State Department during the Clinton and Bush years as a senior official responsible for North Korea policy, told me. "They go nuts when you talk about it."

The camps have barely pricked the world's collective conscience. In the United States, newspaper stories notwithstanding, ignorance of their existence remains widespread. For several years in Washington, a handful of North Korean defectors and camp survivors gathered each spring on the Mall for speeches and marches. The Washington press corps paid little attention. Part of the reason was language. Most of the defectors spoke only Korean. As important, in a media culture that feeds on celebrity, no movie star, no pop idol, no Nobel Prize winner stepped forward to demand that outsiders invest emotionally in a distant issue that lacks good video.

"Tibetans have the Dalai Lama and Richard Gere, Burmese have Aung San Suu Kyi, Darfurians have Mia Farrow and George Clooney," Suzanne Scholte, a long-time activist who brought camp survivors to Washington, told me. "North Koreans have no one like that."

Shin told me he does not deserve to speak for the tens of thousands still in the camps. He is ashamed of what he did to survive and escape. He has resisted learning English, in part because he does not want to have to tell his story again and again in a language that might make him important. But he desperately wants the world to understand what North Korea has tried so diligently to hide. His burden is a heavy one. No one else born and raised in the camps has escaped to explain what went on inside—what still goes on inside.

CHAPTER 1

THE BOY WHO ATE
HIS MOTHER'S LUNCH

Shin and his mother lived in the best prisoner quarters Camp 14 had to offer: a "model village" next to an orchard and just across from the field where his mother was later hanged.

Each of the forty, one-story buildings in the village housed four families. Shin and his mother had their own room, where they slept side by side on a concrete floor. The four families shared a common kitchen, which had a single bare lightbulb. Electricity ran two hours a day, from four to five in the morning and ten to eleven at night. Windows were made of gray vinyl, too opaque to see through. Rooms were heated—in the Korean way—by a coal fire in the kitchen with flues running under the bedroom floor. The camp had its own coal mines and coal for heating was readily available.

There were no beds, chairs, or tables. There was no running water. No bath or shower. Prisoners who wanted to bathe sometimes sneaked down to the river in the summer. About thirty families shared a well for drinking water. They also shared a privy, which was divided in half for men and women. Defecating and urinating there were mandatory, as human waste was used as fertilizer on the camp farm.

If Shin's mother met her daily work quota, she could bring home food for that night and the following day. At four in the morning, she would prepare breakfast and lunch for her son and for herself. Every meal was the same: corn porridge, pickled cabbage, and cabbage soup. Shin ate this meal nearly every day for twenty-three years, unless he was denied food as punishment.

When he was too young for school, his mother often left him alone in the house in the morning, and came back from the fields at midday for lunch. Shin was always hungry and he would eat his lunch as soon as his mother left for work in the morning.

He also ate her lunch.

When she came back at midday and found nothing to eat, she would become furious and beat her son with a hoe, a shovel, anything close at hand. Some of the beatings were as violent as those he later received from guards.

Still, Shin took as much food as he could from his mother as often as he could. It did not occur to him that if he ate her lunch she would go hungry. Many years later, after she was dead and he was living in the United States, he would tell me that he loved his mother. But that was in retrospect. That was after he learned that a civilized child should love his mother. When he was in the camp—depending upon her for all his meals, stealing her food, enduring her beatings—he saw her as competition for survival.

Her name was Jang Hye Gyung. Shin remembers her as short and slightly plump with powerful arms. She wore her hair cut short, like all women in the camp, and was required to cover her head with a white cloth folded into a triangle that tied around the back of her neck. Shin discovered her birth date—October 1, 1950—from a document he saw during his interrogation in the underground prison.

She never talked to him about her past, her family, or why she was in the camp, and he never asked. His existence as her son had been arranged by guards. They chose her and the man who became Shin's father as prizes for each other in a "reward" marriage.

Single men and women slept in dormitories segregated by sex. The eighth rule of Camp 14, as Shin was required to memorize it, said: "Should sexual physical contact occur without prior approval, the perpetrators will be shot immediately."

Rules were the same in other North Korean labor camps. If unauthorized sex resulted in a pregnancy or a birth, the woman and her baby were usually killed, according to my interviews with a former camp guard and several former prisoners. They said that women who had sex with guards in an attempt to get more food or easier work knew that the risks were high. If they became pregnant, they disappeared.

A reward marriage was the only safe way around the no-sex rule. Marriage was dangled in front of prisoners as the ultimate bonus for hard work and reliable snitching. Men became eligible at twenty-five, women at twenty-three. Guards announced marriages three or four times a year, usually on propitious dates, such as New Year's or Kim Jong Il's birthday. Neither bride nor groom had much say in deciding whom they would marry. If one partner found his or her chosen mate to be unacceptably old, cruel, or ugly, guards would sometimes cancel a marriage. If they did, neither the man nor the woman would be allowed to marry again.

Shin's father, Shin Gyung Sub, told Shin that guards gave him Jang as payment for his skill in operating a metal lathe in the camp's machine shop. Shin's mother never told Shin why she had been given the honor of marriage.

But for her, as for many brides in the camp, marriage was a kind of promotion. It came with a slightly better job and better housing—in the model village, where there was a school and health clinic. Shortly after her marriage, she was transferred there from a crowded dormitory for women in the camp's garment factory. Jang was also given a coveted job on a nearby farm, where there were opportunities to steal corn, rice, and green vegetables.

After their marriage, the couple was allowed to sleep together for five consecutive nights. From then on, Shin's father, who continued to live in a dormitory at his work site, was permitted to visit Jang a few times a year. Their liaison produced two sons. The eldest, He Geun, was born in 1974. Shin was born eight years later.

The brothers barely knew each other. When Shin was born, his older brother was away in primary school for ten hours a day. By the time Shin was four, his brother had moved out of the house (at the mandatory age of twelve) and into a dormitory.

As for his father, Shin remembers that he sometimes showed up at night and left early in the morning. He paid little attention to the boy, and Shin grew up indifferent to his presence.

In the years after he escaped the camp, Shin learned that many people associate warmth, security, and affection with the words "mother," "father," and "brother." That was not his experience. Guards taught him and other children in the camp that they were prisoners because of the "sins" of their parents. The children were told that while they should always be ashamed of their traitorous blood, they could go a long way toward "washing away" their inherent sinfulness by working hard, obeying the guards, and informing on their parents. The tenth rule of Camp 14 said that a prisoner "must truly" consider each guard as his teacher. That made sense to Shin. As a child and as a teen, his parents were exhausted, distant, and uncommunicative.

Shin was a scrawny, incurious, and for the most part friendless child whose one source of certainty was the guards' lectures about redemption through snitching. His understanding of right and wrong, though, was often muddied by encounters he witnessed between his mother and camp guards.

When he was ten, Shin left his house one evening and went looking for his mother. He was hungry and it was time for her to prepare dinner. He walked to a nearby rice field where his mother worked and asked a woman if she had seen her.

"She's cleaning the *bowijidowon*'s room," the woman told him, referring to the office of the guard in charge of the rice farm.

Shin walked to the guard's office and found the front door locked. He peeked through a window on the side of the building. His mother was on her knees cleaning the floor. As Shin watched, the *bowijidowon* came into view. He approached Shin's mother from behind and began to grope her. She offered no resistance. Both of them removed their clothes. Shin watched them have sex.

He never asked his mother about what he saw, and never mentioned it to his father.

That same year, students in Shin's class at primary school were required to volunteer to help their parents at work. He joined his mother one morning to plant rice seedlings. She seemed unwell and fell behind in her planting. Shortly before the lunch break, her slack pace caught the eye of a guard.

"You bitch," he shouted at her.

"Bitch" was the standard form of address when camp guards spoke to female prisoners. Guards usually called Shin and other male prisoners "son of a bitch."

"How are you able to stuff your face when you can't even plant rice?" the guard asked.

She apologized, but the guard grew increasingly angry.

"This bitch won't do," he shouted.

As Shin stood beside his mother, the guard invented a punishment for her.

"Go kneel on that ridge there and raise your arms. Stay in that position until I come back from lunch."

Shin's mother knelt on the ridge in the sun for an hour and a half, arms reaching for the sky. The boy stood nearby and watched. He did not know what to say to her. He said nothing.

When the guard returned, he ordered Shin's mother back to work. Weak and hungry, she passed out in the middle of the afternoon. Shin ran to the guard, begging him for help. Other workers dragged his mother to a shaded rest area, where she regained consciousness.

That evening, Shin went with his mother to an "ideological struggle" meeting, a compulsory gathering for self-criticism. Shin's mother again fell to her knees at the meeting, as forty of her fellow farm workers followed the *bowijidowon*'s lead and berated her for failing to fill her work quota.

On summer nights, Shin and some of the other small boys in his village would sneak into the orchard just north of the cluster of concrete dwellings where they lived. They picked unripe pears and cucumbers and ate them as quickly as they could. When they were caught, guards would beat them with batons and ban them from lunch at school for several days.

Guards, though, did not care if Shin and his friends ate rats, frogs, snakes, and insects. They were intermittently abundant in the sprawling camp, which used few pesticides, relied on human waste as fertilizer, and supplied no water for cleaning privies or taking baths.

Eating rats not only filled empty stomachs, it was essential to survival. Their flesh could help prevent pellagra, a sometimes fatal disease that was rampant in the camp, especially in the winter. Prisoners with pellagra, the result of a lack of protein and niacin in their diets, suffered weakness, skin lesions, diarrhea, and dementia. It was a frequent cause of death.

Catching and roasting rats became a passion for Shin. He caught them in his house, in the fields, and in the privy. He would meet his friends in the evening at his primary school, where there was a coal grill to roast them. Shin peeled away their skin, scraped away their innards, salted what was left, and chewed the rest—flesh, bones, and tiny feet.

He also learned to use the stems of foxtail grass to spear grasshoppers, longheaded locusts, and dragonflies, which he roasted over a fire in late summer and autumn. In the mountain forests, where groups of students were often sent to gather wood, Shin ate wild grapes, gooseberries, and Korean raspberries by the fistful.

During winter, spring, and early summer, there was much less to eat. Hunger drove him and his boyhood friends to try strategies that older prisoners in the camp claimed could ease the discomfort of an empty stomach. They ate meals without water or soup, under the theory that liquid accelerated digestion and quickened the return of hunger pangs. They also tried to refrain from defecating, believing that this would make them feel full and less obsessed with food. An alternative hunger-fighting technique was to imitate cows, regurgitating a recent meal and eating it again. Shin tried this a few times, but it didn't help ease his hunger.

Summertime, when children were sent to the fields to help plant and weed, was peak season for rats and field mice. Shin remembers eating them every day. His happiest, most contented childhood moments were when his belly was full.

The "eating problem," as it's often called in North Korea, is not confined to labor camps. It has stunted the bodies of millions across the country.

Teenage boys fleeing the North in the past decade are on average five inches shorter and weigh twenty-five pounds less than boys growing up in South Korea.[1]

Mental retardation caused by early childhood malnutrition disqualifies about a quarter of potential military conscripts in North Korea, according to the National Intelligence Council, a research institution that is part of the U.S. intelligence community. Its report said hunger-caused intellectual disabilities among the young were likely to cripple economic growth even if the country opened to the outside world or united with the South.

Since the 1990s, North Korea has been unable to grow, buy, or deliver enough food to feed its population. Famine in the mid-1990s killed perhaps a million North Koreans. A similar death rate in the United States would claim about twelve million lives.

The North's food disaster eased in the late 1990s as the government agreed to receive international food aid. The United States became North Korea's largest aid donor while remaining its most demonized enemy.

Every year North Korea needs to produce more than five million tons of rice and cereal grain to feed its twenty-three million people. Nearly every year it falls short, usually by about a million tons. With long winters and high mountains, the country lacks arable land, denies incentives to farmers, and cannot afford fuel or modern farm equipment.

It squeaked by for years without a food catastrophe thanks to subsidies from Moscow. When the Soviet Union collapsed, the subsidies ended, and North Korea's centrally planned economy stopped functioning. There was no free fuel for its aging factories, no guaranteed market for its often-shoddy goods, and no access to cheap, Soviet-made chemical fertilizers on which state farms had become dependent.

For several years, South Korea helped fill the gap, giving Pyongyang half a million tons of fertilizer annually as part of its "Sunshine Policy" to try to ease North-South tensions.

When new leadership in Seoul cut off the free fertilizer in 2008, North Korea tried to do nationally what it has been doing for decades in its labor camps. The masses were told to make *toibee*, a fertilizer in which ash is mixed with human excrement. In recent winters, frozen human waste has been chipped out of public toilets in cities and towns across the country. Factories, public enterprises, and neighborhoods have been ordered to produce two tons of *toibee*, according to Good Friends, a Buddhist charity with informants in North Korea. In the spring, it was dried in the open air before being transported to state farms. But organic fertilizers have not come close to replacing the chemicals that state farms depended on for decades.

Sealed away behind an electrified fence during the 1990s, Shin was unaware that millions of his countrymen were desperately hungry.

Neither he nor his parents (as far as Shin knew) heard that the government was struggling to feed the army or that people were dying of starvation in their apartments in North Korean cities, including the capital.

They did not know that tens of thousands of North Koreans had abandoned their homes and were walking into China in search of food. Nor were they beneficiaries of the billions of dollars' worth of food aid that poured into North Korea. During those chaotic years, as the basic functioning of Kim Jong Il's government stalled, think tank experts in the West were writing books with doomsday titles such as *The End of North Korea.*

The end was nowhere in sight inside Camp 14, which was self-sufficient except for occasional trainloads of salt.

Prisoners grew their own corn and cabbage. As slave workers, they produced low-cost vegetables and fruit, farmed fish and pork, and made uniforms, cement, pottery, and glassware for the crumbling economy outside the fence.

Shin and his mother were miserable and hungry during the famine, but no more than they were accustomed to. The boy carried on as before, hunting rats, filching his mother's food, and always enduring her beatings.

CHAPTER 2

SCHOOL DAYS

The teacher sprang a surprise search. He rifled through Shin's pockets and those of the forty other six-year-olds in his class.

When it was over, the teacher held five kernels of corn. They all belonged to a girl who was short, slight, and, as Shin remembers, exceptionally pretty. He doesn't recall the girl's name, but everything else about that school day in June 1989 stands out in his memory.

The teacher was in a bad mood as he began searching pockets. When he found corn, he erupted.

"You bitch, you stole corn? You want your hands cut off?"

He ordered the girl to the front of the class and told her to kneel. Swinging his long wooden pointer, he struck her on the head again and again. As Shin and his classmates watched in silence, lumps puffed up on her skull. Blood leaked from her nose. She toppled over onto the concrete floor. Shin and several other classmates picked her up and carried her home to a pig farm not far from the school. Later that night, she died. Subsection three of Camp 14's third rule said: "Anyone who steals or conceals any foodstuffs will be shot immediately."

Shin had learned that teachers usually did not take this rule seriously. If they found food in a student's pocket, they would sometimes deliver a couple of desultory whacks with a stick. More often they would do nothing. It was common for Shin and other students to take a chance. The pretty little girl was just unlucky, as Shin saw it.

He had been trained by guards and teachers to believe that every time he was beaten, he deserved it—because of the treasonous blood he had inherited from his parents. The girl was no different. Shin thought her punishment was just and fair, and he never became angry with his teacher for killing her. He believed his classmates felt the same way.

At school the next day, no mention was made of the beating. Nothing changed in the classroom. As far as Shin was aware, the teacher was not disciplined for his actions.

Shin spent all five years of primary school in class with this same teacher, who was in his early thirties, wore a uniform, and carried a pistol in a holster on his hip. In breaks between classes, he allowed students to play "rock, paper, scissors." On Saturdays, he would sometime grant children an hour or two to pick lice out of each other's hair. Shin never learned his name.

In grade school Shin was taught to stand up straight, bow to his teachers, and never look them in the eye. At the start of school, he was given a black uniform: pants, shirt, an undershirt, and a pair of shoes. They were replaced every two years, although they began to fall apart within a month or two.

Soap was sometimes distributed to students as a special reward for hard work. Shin did not distinguish himself with diligence and rarely touched soap. His pants were cardboard stiff from dirt and sweat. If he scraped his skin with a fingernail, grime flaked off. When it was too cold to bathe in the river or stand outside in the rain, Shin and his mother and his classmates smelled like farm animals. Nearly everyone's kneecaps turned black in winter from the dirt. Shin's mother sewed underwear and socks for him out of rags. After her death, he wore no underwear and struggled to find rags to wear inside his shoes.

School, a cluster of buildings readily viewed on satellite photographs, was about a seven-minute walk from Shin's house. Windows there were made of glass, not vinyl. That was the only frill. Like his mother's house, Shin's classroom was made of concrete. The teacher stood at a podium in front of a single blackboard. Boys and girls sat separately on either side of a middle aisle. Portraits of Kim Il Sung and Kim Jong Il—the centerpieces of every classroom in North Korea—were nowhere to be found.

Instead, the school taught rudimentary literacy and numeracy, drilled children in camp rules, and constantly reminded them of their iniquitous blood. Primary school students attended class six days a week. Secondary students attended seven, with one day off a month.

"You have to wash away the sins of your mothers and fathers, so work hard!" the headmaster told them at assemblies.

The school day began promptly at eight with a session called *chonghwa*. It means total harmony, but it was an occasion for the teacher to criticize students for what they had done wrong the previous day. Attendance was checked twice daily. No matter how sick a student might be, absences were not allowed. Shin occasionally helped his classmates carry an ailing student to school. But he was rarely sick, other than with colds. He was inoculated just once, for smallpox.

Shin learned how to read and write the Korean alphabet, doing exercises on coarse paper made in the camp from cornhusks. Each term, he was given one notebook with twenty-five pages. For a pencil, he often used a sharpened shaft of charred wood. He did not know of the existence of erasers. There were no reading exercises, as the teacher had the only book. For writing exercises, students were instructed to explain how they had failed to work hard and follow rules.

Shin learned to add and subtract, but not to multiply and divide. To this day, when he needs to multiply, he adds a column of numbers.

Physical education meant running around outside and playing on iron bars in the schoolyard. Sometimes, students would go down to the river and gather snails for their teacher. There were no ball games. Shin saw a soccer ball for the first time when he was twenty-three, after fleeing to China.

The school's long-term goals for students were implicit in what teachers never bothered to teach. They told Shin that North Korea was an independent state and noted the existence of cars and trains. (This wasn't much of a revelation, since Shin had seen guards drive cars and there was a train station in the southwest corner of the camp.) But teachers said nothing about North Korea's geography, its neighbors, its history, or its leaders. Shin had only a vague notion of who the Great Leader and the Dear Leader were.

Questions were not allowed in school. They angered teachers and triggered beatings. Teachers talked; students listened. By repetition in class, Shin mastered the alphabet and basic grammar. He learned how to pronounce words, but frequently had no idea what they meant. His teacher made him afraid, on an instinctive level, of trying to seek out new information.

Shin never came in contact with a classmate who had been born outside the camp. As far as he could tell, the school was reserved for children like him, the camp-bred spawn of reward marriages. He was told that children born elsewhere and brought into the camp with their parents were denied schooling and confined to the camp's most remote sections, Valleys 4 and 5.

His teachers, as a result, could shape the minds and values of students without contradiction from children who might know something about what existed beyond the fence.

There was no secret about what was in store for Shin and his classmates. Primary and secondary school trained them for hard labor. In the winter, children cleared snow, chopped down trees, and shoveled coal for heating the school. The entire student body (about a thousand students) was mobilized to clean privies in the Bowiwon village where guards lived, some of them with wives and children. Shin and his classmates went from house to house chipping out frozen feces with hoes and dumping the waste with bare hands (there were no gloves for camp prisoners) on A-frame racks. They dragged the excrement to surrounding fields or carried it on their backs.

On warmer, happier days, after school ended in the afternoon, Shin's class would sometimes march into the hills and mountains behind the school to collect food and herbs for their guards. Although it was against the rules, they often stuffed bracken, osmunda, and other ferns inside their uniforms and brought them home to their mothers to make side dishes. They picked agaric mushrooms in April and pine mushrooms in October. On these long afternoon walks, children were allowed to talk with each other. Strict segregation between sexes was relaxed, as boys and girls worked, giggled, and played alongside one another.

Shin began first grade with two other children from his village—Hong Sung Jo, a boy, and Moon Sung Sim, a girl. They walked to school together for five years and sat in the same classroom. In secondary school, they spent another five years in one another's company.

Shin viewed Hong Sung Jo as his closest companion. They played jacks between classes at school. Their mothers worked at the same farm. Neither boy, though, ever invited the other to his house to play.

Trust among friends was poisoned by constant competition for food and pressure to snitch. Trying to win extra food rations, children told teachers and guards what their neighbors were eating, wearing, and saying.

Collective punishment at school also turned classmates against each other. Shin's class was often given a daily quota of trees to plant or acorns to gather. If they failed to meet expectations, everyone in his class was penalized. Teachers ordered Shin's class to give up its lunch ration (for a day or sometimes a week) to another class that had filled its quota. In work details, Shin was usually slow, often last.

As Shin and his classmates grew older, their work details, called "rallies of endeavor," grew longer and more difficult. During "weeding combat," which occurred between June and August, primary school students worked from four in the morning until dusk pulling weeds in corn, bean, and sorghum fields.

When Shin and his classmates entered secondary school, they were barely literate. But by then classroom instruction had come to an end. Teachers became foremen. Secondary school was a staging ground for work details in mines, fields, and forests. At the end of the day, it was a gathering place for long sessions of self-criticism.

Shin entered his first coal mine at the age of ten. He and five of his classmates (three boys and three girls, including his neighbor Moon Sung Sim) walked down a steep shaft to the face of the mine. Their job was to load coal into two-ton ore cars and push them uphill on a narrow rail track to a staging area. To meet their daily quota, they had to get four cars up the hill.

The first two took all morning. After a lunch of milled corn and salted cabbage, the exhausted children, their faces and clothes covered in coal dust, headed back to the coalface, carrying candles in the ink-black mine.

One day, pushing the third car, Moon Sung Sim lost her balance and one of her feet slipped beneath a steel wheel. Shin, who was standing next to her, heard a scream. He tried to help the writhing, sweating girl remove her shoe. Her big toe was crushed and oozing blood. Another student tied a shoelace around her ankle as a kind of tourniquet.

Shin and two other boys lifted Moon into an empty coal car and pushed it to the top of the mine. Then they carried her to the camp hospital, where her mangled toe was amputated without anesthetics and treated with salt water.

In addition to harder physical work, secondary school students spent more time finding fault with themselves and one another. They wrote in their cornhusk notebooks, preparing for the self-censure sessions that took place after the evening meal. About ten students a night had to admit to something.

Shin tried to meet with his classmates before these sessions to sort out who would confess to what. They invented sins that would satisfy teachers without provoking draconian punishment. Shin remembers confessing to eating corn he found on the ground and to taking a cat-nap when no one was looking. If students volunteered enough transgressions, punishments were usually a smack on the head and a warning to work harder.

Wedged closely together, twenty-five boys slept on the concrete floor in the secondary school dormitory. The strongest boys slept near—but not too near—a coal-heated flue that ran under the floor. Weaker boys, including Shin, slept farther away and often shivered through the night. Some had no choice but to try to sleep on top of the flue, where they risked severe burns when the heating system flared up.

Shin remembers a stoutly built, prideful twelve-year-old named

Ryu Hak Chul. He slept wherever he chose, and he was also the only boy who dared sass a teacher.

Ryu ditched his work assignment one day, and his disappearance was quickly reported. His teacher sent Shin's class to find the missing boy.

"Why'd you stop working and run away?" the teacher asked when Ryu had been found and marched back to school.

To Shin's astonishment, Ryu did not apologize.

"I got hungry, so I went to eat," he said flatly.

The teacher, too, was astonished.

"Is this son of a bitch talking back?" the teacher asked.

He ordered students to tie Ryu to a tree. They took off his shirt and bound him with wire.

"Beat him until he comes to his senses," the teacher said.

Without a second thought, Shin joined his classmates in thrashing Ryu.

CHAPTER 3

THE UPPER CRUST

Shin was nine years old when the North Korean caste system knocked him on the head.

He and about thirty of his classmates were walking in early spring toward the train station, where their teacher had sent them to pick up coal that had spilled from railroad cars during loading. The station is near the southwestern corner of Camp 14, and to get there from school students had to pass below the Bowiwon compound, which sits on a bluff above the Taedong River. Children of guards live in the compound and attend school there.

From up above, the guards' children shouted at Shin and his classmates as they walked by.

"Reactionary sons of bitches are coming."

Rocks the size of fists rained down on the prison children. With the river below and the bluff above, they had no place to hide. A rock hit Shin in the face, just below his left eye, opening up a deep cut. Shin and his classmates shrieked and cowered on the dirt road, trying to protect their heads with their arms and hands.

A second rock struck Shin in the head, knocking him to the ground and making him dizzy. When his head cleared, the stoning had stopped.

Many of his classmates were moaning and bleeding. Moon, his neighbor and classmate who later lost her big toe in the mine, had been knocked out. The leader of Shin's class, Hong Joo Hyun, who was supposed to be a kind of foreman for the day's work mission, was also out cold.

Earlier that morning at school, their teacher had told them to hurry ahead to the train station and start work. He said he would catch up later.

When the teacher finally walked down the road and discovered his bloodied students sprawled in the road, he became angry.

"What are you doing not getting yourselves to work?" he shouted.

Students timidly asked what they should do with classmates who were still unconscious.

"Put them on your backs and carry them," the teacher instructed. "All you need to do is work hard."

In the years ahead, when Shin spotted Bowiwon children anywhere in the camp, he walked in the opposite direction if he could.

Bowiwon children had every reason to throw stones at the likes of Shin. His blood, as that of the offspring of irredeemable sinners, was tainted in the worst conceivable way. Bowiwon children, however, came from families whose lineage had been sanctified by the Great Leader.

To identify and isolate his perceived political enemies, Kim Il Sung created a neofeudal, blood-based pecking order in 1957. The government classified and, to a considerable extent, segregated the entire North Korean population based on the perceived reliability of an individual's parents and grandparents. North Korea called itself the Worker's Paradise, but even as it professed allegiance to communist ideals of equality, it invented one of the world's most rigidly stratified caste systems.

Three broad classes were created, with fifty-one subgroups. At the top, members of the core class could obtain jobs in government, the Korean Workers' Party, officer ranks of the military, and the intelligence services. The core class included farm workers, families of soldiers killed during the Korean War, families of troops who had served with Kim Il Sung fighting against Japanese occupation, and government workers.

The next level was the wavering or neutral class, which included soldiers, technicians, and teachers. At the bottom was the hostile class, whose members were suspected of opposing the government. They included former property owners, relatives of Koreans who had fled to South Korea, Christians, and those who worked for the Japanese colonial government that controlled the Korean Peninsula before World War II. Their descendants now work in mines and factories. They are not allowed into universities.

Besides dictating career opportunities, the system shaped geographic destiny, with the core class allowed to live in and around Pyongyang. Many members of the hostile class were resettled to distant provinces along the Chinese border. Some members of the wavering class could move up in the system by joining the Korean People's Army, serving with distinction and, with luck and connections, securing a lower rung in the ruling party.

Also, rapid growth of private markets made some traders from the wavering and hostile classes wealthy, allowing them to buy and bribe their way into better living standards than some of the political elite.[1]

For government positions, though, family background decided nearly everything—including who had the right to throw stones at Shin.

The only North Koreans considered trustworthy enough to become guards in political prison camps were men like An Myeong Chul, the son of a North Korean intelligence officer.

He was recruited into the Bowibu at nineteen, after two years of military service. As part of the process, the loyalty of his entire extended family was checked. He was also required to sign a document saying he would never disclose the existence of the camps. Sixty percent of the two hundred young men who were recruited with him as guards were also the sons of intelligence officers.

An worked as a guard and driver in four labor camps (not including Camp 14) for seven years in the late 1980s and early 1990s. He fled to China in 1994, after his father, who supervised regional food distribution, ran afoul of his superiors and committed suicide. After finding his way to South Korea, An found work as a banker in Seoul and married a South Korean woman. They have two children. He also became a human rights activist.

After his defection, he learned that his sister and brother were sent to a labor camp, where his brother later died.

When we spoke over a Chinese dinner in Seoul in 2009, An wore a dark blue suit, a white shirt, a striped tie, and half-frame glasses. He looked prosperous and spoke in a quiet, careful way. Still, he is a man of intimidating size, with large hands and linebacker shoulders.

When he was training to be a guard, he studied the Korean martial art of taekwondo, learned riot-suppression techniques, and was instructed not to worry if his treatment of prisoners caused injury or death. In the camps, he became accustomed to hitting prisoners who did not meet work quotas. He remembers beating up a hunchbacked prisoner.

"It was normal to beat prisoners," he said, explaining that his instructors taught him never to smile and to think of inmates as "dogs and pigs."

"We were taught not to think of them as human beings," he said. "The instructors told us not to show pity. They said, 'If you do, you will become a prisoner.'"

Although pity was forbidden, there were few other guidelines for treatment of prisoners. As a result, An said, guards were free to indulge their appetites and eccentricities, often preying on attractive young women prisoners, who would usually consent to sex for better treatment.

"If this resulted in babies, women and their babies were killed," An said, noting that he had personally seen newborns clubbed to death with iron rods. "The theory behind the camps was to cleanse unto three generations the families of incorrect thinkers. So it was inconsistent to allow another generation to be born."

Guards could win admission to college if they caught an inmate trying to escape—an incentive system that ambitious guards seized upon. They would enable prisoners to make an escape attempt, An said, and shoot them before they reached the fences that surround the camps.

Most often though, An said, prisoners were beaten, sometimes to death, simply because guards were bored or in a sour mood.

Although prison guards and their legitimate children belong by blood to the core class, they are fringe functionaries locked away for most of their working lives in the freezing hinterlands.

The core of the core lives in Pyongyang in large apartments or single-family homes in gated neighborhoods. Outsiders do not know with any certainty how many of these elite there are in North Korea, but South Korean and American scholars believe they are a tiny fraction of the country's population, numbering between 100,000 and 200,000 out of 23 million.

Trusted and talented members of the elite are periodically allowed outside the country, where they serve as diplomats and traders for state-owned companies. In the past decade, the United States government and law enforcement agencies around the world have documented that some of these North Koreans are involved in criminal enterprises that funnel hard currency to Pyongyang.

They have been linked to counterfeiting $100 bills, cyberterrorism, trafficking drugs ranging from heroin to Viagra, and marketing high-quality brand-name (but counterfeit) cigarettes. In violation of United Nations resolutions, North Koreans have also sold rockets and nuclear weapons technology to countries including Iran and Syria, according to U.N. officials.

One well-traveled member of the North Korean elite told me how he earned his keep while securing the support and affections of Kim Jong Il.

His name is Kim Kwan Jin and he grew up in Pyongyang as a member of the blue-blood elite. He studied British literature at Kim Il Sung University, which is reserved for children of top officials. His professional expertise—before defecting to South Korea in 2003—was managing a state-run global insurance fraud. It collected hundreds of millions of dollars from some of the world's largest insurance companies on falsified claims for industrial accidents and natural disasters inside North Korea. And it funneled most of the money to the Dear Leader.

The festive annual highlight of this scheme took place in the week before Kim Jong Il's birthday on February 16. Foreign-based executives of the Korean National Insurance Corporation, the state monopoly that orchestrated the fraud, prepared a special birthday gift.

From his office in Singapore, Kim Kwan Jin watched in early February 2003 as his colleagues stuffed twenty million dollars in cash into two heavy-duty bags and sent them, via Beijing, to Pyongyang. This was money that had been paid by international insurance companies, and it was not a one-time offering. Kim said that in the five years he was based in Pyongyang for the state insurance corporation, bags of cash always arrived in time for his leader's birthday. He said they came from Switzerland, France, and Austria, as well as from Singapore.

The money, he said, was delivered to Office 39 of the Korean Workers' Party Central Committee. This infamous office or bureau was created by Kim Jong Il in the 1970s to collect hard currency and to give him a power base independent of his father, who was then still running the country. According to Kim (and scores of other defectors and published accounts), Office 39 buys luxury goods to secure the loyalty of the North Korean elite. It also funds the purchase of foreign-made components for missiles and other weapons programs.

As Kim explained it to me, his country's insurance scam worked like this: Pyongyang-based managers for the state insurance monopoly would write policies that covered costly but common North Korean disasters such as mining accidents, train crashes, and crop losses resulting from floods. "The major point of the reinsurance operation is that they are banking on disaster," he said. "Whenever there is a disaster, it becomes a source of hard currency" for the government.

Kim and other foreign-based operatives of the North Korean insurance company were dispatched around the globe to find insurance brokers who would accept seductively high insurance premiums to compensate North Korea for the cost of these disasters.

Reinsurance is a multibillion-dollar industry that spreads the risk assumed by one insurance company to a number of companies around the world. Each year, Kim said, North Korea would do its best to shuffle its offerings among the major reinsurance players.

"We pass it around," he told me. "One year, it might be Lloyd's [of London]. The next year, it might be Swiss Re."

By spreading relatively moderate losses among many big companies, North Korea concealed how bad a risk it was. Its government prepared meticulously documented claims, rushed them through its puppet court, and demanded immediate payment. But it often restricted the ability of reinsurers to dispatch investigators to verify claims. According to a London-based expert on the insurance industry, North Korea also exploited the geographical ignorance and political naïveté of some reinsurers and their brokers. Many of them thought they were dealing with a firm from South Korea, the expert said, while others were unaware that North Korea is a closed totalitarian state with sham courts and no international accountability.

Over time, reinsurance companies got wise to frequent and costly claims for train crashes and ferry sinkings that were all but impossible to investigate. Lawyers for German insurance giant Allianz Global Investors, Lloyd's of London, and several other reinsurers filed suit in a London court against the Korean National Insurance Corporation. They contested its claim for a 2005 crash of a helicopter into a government-owned warehouse in Pyongyang. In court documents, the companies alleged that the crash was staged, that the North Korean court's decision to uphold the claim had been rigged, and that North Korea routinely used insurance fraud to raise money for the personal use of Kim Jong Il.

The reinsurance companies, however, dropped their claims and agreed to a settlement that was a near-complete victory for North Korea. They did so, legal analysts said, because they had foolishly signed contracts in which they agreed to be bound by North Korean law. After the settlement, North Korea's lawyers said it was "staggeringly unfair" to suggest that the country engaged in insurance fraud. But publicity generated by the case alerted the world's reinsurance industry to avoid North Korea, and fraud wound down.

When Kim Kwang Jin helped send the twenty-million-dollar bags of cash from Singapore to Pyongyang, he said that Kim Jong Il was delighted.

"We received a letter of thanks and it was a great celebration," he said, noting that Kim Jong Il arranged for him and his colleagues to receive gifts that included oranges, apples, DVD players, and blankets.

Fruit, home electronics, and blankets.

This meager display of dictatorial gratitude is telling. In Pyongyang, living standards for the core class are luxurious only by the standards of a country where a third of the population is chronically hungry.

Elites have relatively large apartments and access to rice. They are also granted first dibs on imported luxuries such as fruit and liquor. But for residents of Pyongyang, electricity is intermittent at best, hot water is rarely available, and travel outside the country is difficult except for diplomats and state-sponsored businessmen.

"An elite family in Pyongyang does not live nearly as well—in terms of material possessions, creature comforts, and entertainment options—as the family of an average salaryman in Seoul," Andrei Lankov, a Russian-born political scientist who attended college in Pyongyang and now teaches at Kookmin University in Seoul, told me. Average per capita income in South Korea is fifteen times as high as in the North ($1,900 in 2009). Countries with higher per capita incomes than North Korea include Sudan, Congo, and Laos.

The exception, of course, is the Kim family dynasty. Satellite images of the family's residences stand out like sable-clad thumbs in the mangy landscape of North Korea. The family maintains at least eight country houses, according to books by his former chef and a former bodyguard. Nearly all of them have movie theaters, basketball courts, and shooting ranges. Several have indoor swimming pools, along with entertainment centers for bowling and roller skating. Satellite pictures show a full-size horseracing track, a private train station, and a water park.

A private yacht, which has a fifty-meter pool with two waterslides, was photographed near the family's house in Wonsan, which is located on a peninsula with white sandy beaches and is believed to be a family favorite. The former bodyguard said Kim Jong Il often went there to hunt roe deer, pheasants, and wild geese. All his houses have been furnished with imports from Japan and Europe. The family's beef is raised by bodyguards on a special cattle ranch, and their apples come from an organic orchard where sugar, a rare and costly commodity in the North, is added to the soil to sweeten the fruit.[2]

The privileges of blood are uniquely rich in the Kim family. Kim Jong Il inherited his dictatorial control of North Korea from his father in 1994—the first hereditary succession in the communist world. The second such succession occurred in December 2011, after Kim's death at age sixty-nine. His youngest son, Kim Jong Eun, was promptly hailed as the "supreme leader" of the party, state, and army. Although it was unclear if he, his older relatives, or the generals would wield real power, propagandists worked overtime manufacturing a new cult of personality. Kim Jong Eun was described in the party daily, *Rodong Sinmun*, as "the spiritual pillar and lighthouse of hope" for the military and the people. The state news agency noted that the new leader is "a prominent thinker-theoretician and peerlessly illustrious commander" who will be a "solid foundation for the prosperity of the country."

Other than having the right blood, the son's qualifications were meager. He attended a German-language school in Liebefeld, Switzerland, where he played point guard on the basketball team and spent hours making pencil drawings of Chicago Bulls great Michael Jordan.[3] He returned to Pyongyang at seventeen to attend Kim Il Sung University. Little is known about what he studied there.

Preparations for a second father-to-son transfer of power became apparent in Pyongyang shortly after Kim Jong Il suffered a stroke in 2008. It left the Dear Leader with a noticeable limp and signaled the emergence of Kim Jong Eun from obscurity.

In lectures delivered to select audiences in Pyongyang in 2009, Kim Jong Eun was described as a "genius of the literary arts" and a patriot who "is working without sleep or rest" to promote North Korea as a nuclear superpower. A propaganda song, "Footsteps," was circulated at military bases to prepare the cadre for the coming of a dynamic "Young General." He was indeed young, in his late twenties, born in either 1983 or 1984.

At his coming-out party in September 2010, the Young General's face was officially shown to the world for the first time. He was the spitting image of his late grandfather Kim Il Sung, who was always more beloved than Kim Jong Il.

That uncanny resemblance, as Kim Jong Eun moved to consolidate power after the death of his father, seemed orchestrated. His clothes and haircut—Mao suits and a short military trim with no sideburns—were the same as his grandfather's when he seized control of North Korea in 1945. Rumors circulated in South Korea that the resemblance had been enhanced by plastic surgeons in Pyongyang to render the young man as a kind of Great Leader II.

If the new leader is to secure the same steely grip on the country as his father and grandfather, he certainly needs some measure of public support, along with solid backing from the military. His father, Kim Jong Il, might never have been popular, but he had nearly twenty years to learn how to dominate his elders. He had handpicked many of the leading generals and was effectively running the country when his father died in 1994.

Not yet thirty years old, with less than three years to learn the levers, Kim Jong Eun has no such advantage. Until he figures it out, he will have to depend on his privileged blood, a budding cult of personality, and the loyalty of relatives, courtiers, and generals who may or may not be content to stand in the shadows.

CHAPTER 4

MOTHER TRIES TO ESCAPE

Shin was putting on his shoes in the school dormitory when his teacher came looking for him. It was Saturday morning, April 6, 1996.

"Hey, Shin, come out as you are," the teacher said.

Puzzled as to why he had been summoned, Shin hurried out of the dormitory and into the schoolyard. There, three uniformed men were waiting for him beside a jeep. They handcuffed him, blindfolded him with a strip of black cloth, and pushed him into the backseat of the jeep. Without saying a word, they drove him away.

Shin had no idea where he was being taken or why. But after a half hour of bouncing along in the backseat, he became afraid and began to tremble.

When the jeep stopped, the men lifted Shin out and stood him on his feet. He heard the clunk of a heavy metal door opening and closing, then the whine of machinery. Guards nudged him into an elevator, and he felt himself descending. He had entered an underground prison inside the camp.

After stepping out of the elevator, he was led down a corridor and into a large, bare, windowless room where guards removed his blindfold. Opening his eyes, he saw a military officer with four stars pinned to his uniform. The officer sat behind a desk. Two other guards in khaki stood nearby. One of them ordered Shin to sit down in a straight-backed chair.

"You're Shin In Geun?" the officer with four stars asked.

"Yes, that is correct," Shin replied.

"Shin Gyung Sub is the name of your father?"

"Yes."

"Jang Hye Gyung is your mother's name?"

"Yes."

"Shin He Geun is the name of your brother?"

"Yes."

The officer stared at Shin for about five minutes. Shin could not figure out where the interrogation was headed.

"Do you know why you're here?" the officer asked at last.

"I don't know."

"Shall I tell you then?"

Shin nodded yes.

"At dawn today, your mother and your brother were caught trying to escape. That's why you're here. Understand? Were you aware of this fact or not?"

"I . . . I didn't know."

Shin was so shocked by the news that he found it difficult to speak. He wasn't sure if he was awake or dreaming. The officer became increasingly angry and incredulous.

"How is it possible for you not to know that your mother and brother tried to run away?" he asked. "If you want to live, you should spit out the truth."

"No, I really didn't know," Shin said.

"And your father didn't mention anything?"

"It's been a while since I was last home," Shin replied. "When I visited a month ago, I heard nothing."

"What kind of grievance does your family have to risk an escape?" the officer asked.

"I honestly don't know anything."

This was the story that Shin told when he arrived in South Korea in the late summer of 2006. He told it consistently, he told it often, and he told it well.

His debriefings in Seoul began with agents from the government's National Intelligence Service (NIS). Experienced interrogators, they conduct extensive interviews with every North Korean defector and have been trained to screen out the assassins that Kim Jong Il's government periodically dispatched to the South.

After the NIS, Shin told his story to counselors and psychiatrists at a government center for resettlement, then to human rights activists and fellow defectors, and then to the local and international news media. He wrote about it in his 2007 Korean-language memoir, and he told it to me when we first met in December 2008. He elaborated on it nine months later during a week of daylong interviews with me in Seoul.

There was, of course, no way to confirm what he was saying. Shin was the only available source of information about his early life. His mother and brother were dead. His father was still in the camp or perhaps dead too. The North Korean government could hardly set the record straight, since it denies that Camp 14 exists.

Still, the story had been vetted and rang true to survivors of other labor camps, to scholars, to human rights advocates, and to the South Korean government. I believed it and put it in the story that appeared in the *Washington Post*. I wrote that since his mother had not told him about the escape plan, Shin "was startled to hear of it."

———

On a cloudless morning in Torrance, California, Shin revisited and revised the story.

We had been working on the book on and off for about a year, and for the past week we had been sitting across from each other in my dimly lighted room in a Best Western hotel, slowly sifting through the events of his early life.

A day before this session, Shin said he had something new and important to disclose. He insisted that we find a new translator. He also invited Hannah Song, his then-boss and de facto guardian, to listen in. Song was the executive director of Liberty in North Korea, the human rights group that had helped bring him to the United States. A twenty-nine-year-old Korean American, she helped Shin manage his money, visas, travel, medical care, and behavior. She jokingly described herself as Shin's mom.

Shin took off his sandals and tucked his bare feet underneath him on the hotel sofa. I turned on a tape recorder. The sound of morning traffic filtered into the room from Torrance Boulevard. Shin fidgeted with the buttons on his mobile phone.

"So what's up?" I asked.

Shin said he had been lying about his mother's escape. He invented the lie just before arriving in South Korea.

"There were a lot of things I needed to hide," he said. "I was terrified of a backlash, of people asking me, 'Are you even human?'

"It has been a burden to keep this inside. In the beginning, I didn't think much of my lie. It was my intent to lie. Now the people around me make me want to be honest. They make me want to be more moral. In that sense, I felt like I need to tell the truth. I now have friends who are honest. I have begun to understand what honesty is. I feel extreme guilt for everything.

"I was more faithful to guards than to my family. We were each other's spies. I know by telling the truth, people will look down on me.

"Outsiders have a wrong understanding of the camp. It is not just the soldiers who beat us. It is the prisoners themselves who are not kind to each other. There is no sense of community. I am one of those mean prisoners."

Shin said he did not expect forgiveness for what he was about to disclose. He said he had not forgiven himself. He also seemed to be trying to do something more than expiate guilt. He wanted to explain—in a way that he acknowledged would damage his credibility as a witness—how the camp had warped his character.

He said that if outsiders could understand what political prison camps have done—and are doing—to children born inside the fence, it would redeem his lie and his life.

CHAPTER 5

MOTHER TRIES TO ESCAPE, VERSION TWO

This story begins a day earlier, on the afternoon of Friday, April 5, 1996.

As school wound down for the day, Shin's teacher surprised him. He told Shin that he did not have to spend the night in the dormitory. He could go home and eat supper with his mother.

The teacher was rewarding Shin for good behavior. After two years in the dormitory, he had begun to figure a few things out. He was less often a laggard, less often beaten, more often a snitch.

Shin did not particularly want to spend the night at his mother's place. Living apart had not improved their relationship. He still didn't trust her to take care of him; she still seemed tense in his presence. The teacher, however, told him to go home. So he went.

As unexpected as it had been for him to be sent home, there was a bigger surprise when Shin got there. His brother, He Geun, had come home too. He worked at the camp's cement factory, located several miles away in the far southeast of the camp. Shin barely knew and rarely saw He Geun, who had been out of the house for a decade and was now twenty-one.

All that Shin knew about his brother was that he was not a hard worker. He had rarely been granted permission to leave the factory to see his parents. For him to be in his mother's house, Shin thought, he must have finally done something right.

Shin's mother was not delighted when her youngest son showed up unexpectedly for supper. She did not say welcome or that she had missed him.

"Oh, you are home," she said.

Then she cooked, using her daily ration of seven hundred grams of corn meal to make porridge in the one pot she owned. With bowls and spoons, she and her sons ate on the kitchen floor. After he had eaten, Shin went to sleep in the bedroom.

Voices from the kitchen woke him up. He peeked through the bedroom door, curious about what his mother and brother were up to.

His mother was cooking rice. For Shin, this was a slap in the face. He had been served a watery corn soup, the same tasteless gruel he had eaten every day of his life. Now his brother was getting rice.

It is difficult to overstate the importance of rice in North Korean culture. It signifies wealth, evokes the closeness of family, and sanctifies a proper meal. Labor camp prisoners almost never eat rice and its absence is a daily reminder of the normality they can never have.

Outside the camp, too, chronic shortages have removed rice from the daily diets of many North Koreans, especially those in the hostile classes. Teenage defectors from the North, when they arrive in South Korea, have told government counselors of a recurring dream: they are sitting at a table with their families, eating warm rice. Among the elite in Pyongyang, one of the most coveted signifiers of status is an electric rice cooker.

As Shin watched his mother cook, he guessed she must have stolen the rice, a few grains at a time, from the farm where she worked and secreted it away in her house.

In the bedroom, Shin fumed.

He also listened.

His brother was doing most of the talking. Shin heard that He Geun had not been given the day off. Without permission, he had walked away from the cement factory, where he had apparently done something wrong.

Shin realized his brother was in trouble and that he would probably be punished when guards caught up with him. His mother and brother were discussing what they should do.

Escape.

Shin was astonished to hear the word. His brother said it. He was planning to run. His mother was helping him. Her precious hoard of rice was food for flight.

Shin did not hear his mother say that she intended to go along. But she was not trying to argue her eldest into staying, even though she knew that if he escaped or died trying she and others in her family would be tortured and probably killed. Every prisoner knew the first rule of Camp 14, subsection 2: "Any witness to an attempted escape who fails to report it will be shot immediately."

His mother did not sound alarmed. But Shin was. His heart pounded. He was angry that she would put his life at risk for the sake of his older brother. He was afraid he would be implicated in the escape—and shot.

He was also jealous that his brother was getting rice.

On the floor of his mother's bedroom, as the aggrieved thirteen-year-old struggled to contain his fear, Shin's camp-bred instincts took over: he had to tell a guard. He got up off the floor, went into the kitchen, and headed out the door.

"Where are you going?" his mother asked.

"To the toilet," he said.

Shin ran back to his school. It was one in the morning. He entered the school dormitory. His teacher had gone home to the gated Bowi-won village.

Whom could he tell?

In the crowded dormitory room where his class slept, Shin found his friend Hong Sung Jo and woke him up.

As much as Shin trusted anyone, he trusted this boy.

Shin told him what his mother and brother were planning and asked for advice. Hong told him to tell the school's night guard. They went together. As they walked to the guard's office in the main school building, Shin thought of a way to profit from his information.

The guard was awake and in uniform. He told both boys to come inside his office.

"I need to say something to you," Shin told the guard, whom he did not know. "But before I do, I want to get something in return."

The guard assured Shin that he would help.

"I want a guarantee of more food," Shin said.

Shin's second demand was that he be named grade leader at school, a position that would allow him to work less and not be beaten as often.

The guard guaranteed Shin that his requests would be granted.

Accepting the guard's word, Shin explained what his brother and mother were planning and where they were. The guard telephoned his superiors. He told Shin and Hong to go back to the dormitory and get some sleep. He would take care of everything.

On the morning after he betrayed his mother and brother, uniformed men did come to the schoolyard for Shin.

Just as he wrote in his memoir, just as he told everyone in South

Korea, he was handcuffed, blindfolded, pushed into the backseat of a jeep, and driven away in silence to an underground prison inside the camp.

But Shin knew why he had been summoned. And the guards in charge of Camp 14, he expected, knew he had tipped them off.

CHAPTER 6

THIS SON OF A BITCH WON'T DO

"**D**o you know why you are here?"

Shin knew what he had done; he had followed camp rules and stopped an escape.

But the officer did not know—or did not care—that Shin had been a dutiful informer.

"At dawn today, your mother and your brother were caught trying to escape. That's why you're here. Understand? Were you aware of this fact or not? How is it possible for you not to know that your mother and brother tried to run away? If you want to live, you should spit out the truth."

Confused and increasingly frightened, Shin found it difficult to speak. He was an informant. He could not understand why he was being interrogated as an accomplice.

Shin would eventually figure out that the night guard at the school had claimed all the credit for discovering the escape plan. In reporting to his superiors, he had not mentioned Shin's role.

But on that morning in the underground prison, Shin understood nothing. He was a bewildered thirteen-year-old. The officer with four stars kept asking him about the whys, whens, and hows of his family's escape plan. Shin was unable to say anything coherent.

Finally, the officer pushed some papers across his desk.

"In that case, bastard, read this and affix your thumbprint at the bottom."

The document was a family rap sheet. It listed the names, ages, and crimes of Shin's father and of his father's eleven brothers.

The eldest brother, Shin Tae Sub, was listed first. Next to his name was a date: 1951, the second year of the Korean War. On the same line, Shin saw his uncle's crimes: disruption of public peace, acts of brutality, and defection to the South. The same offenses were listed beside the name of Shin's second oldest uncle.

It took Shin many months to understand what he had been allowed to see. The papers explained why his father's family had been locked up in Camp 14.

The unforgivable crime Shin's father had committed was being the brother of two young men who had fled south during a fratricidal war that razed much of the Korean Peninsula and divided hundreds of thousands of families. Shin's unforgivable crime was being his father's son. Shin's father had never explained any of this.

His father later told Shin about the day in 1965 when the family was taken away by security forces. Before dawn, they forced their way into a house owned by Shin's grandfather in Mundok County in South Pyongan Province. It's a fertile farming area located about thirty-five miles north of Pyongyang. "Pack your things," the armed men shouted. They did not explain why the family was being arrested or where they were going. At daybreak, a truck showed up for their belongings. The family traveled for an entire day (a distance of about forty-five miles on mountain roads) before arriving at Camp 14.

———

As ordered, Shin put his thumbprint on the document.

Guards blindfolded him again, led him out of the interrogation room, and marched him down a corridor. When they pulled away the blindfold, Shin read the number "7" on a cell door. Guards pushed him inside and tossed him a prison uniform.

"Hey, son of a bitch, change into this."

The uniform fit a large adult. When Shin pulled it over his short, bony frame, he disappeared into what felt like a burlap sack.

Shin's cell was a concrete square, barely large enough for him to lie down. It had a toilet in the corner and a sink with running water. The lightbulb hanging from the ceiling was on when Shin entered the cell and it could not be turned off. Without windows, Shin could not distinguish night from day. There were two thin blankets on the floor. He was given nothing to eat and could not sleep.

He believes it was the next day when guards opened the door, blindfolded him, and led him to a second interrogation room, where two new officers were waiting. They ordered Shin to kneel and pressed him to explain why his family wanted to escape. What grudges did his mother harbor? What did he discuss with her? What were his brother's intentions?

Shin said he did not have answers to their questions.

"You haven't lived but a few years," one of the guards told Shin. "Just confess and go out and live. Would you like to die in here?"

"I . . . really don't know anything," he replied.

He was increasingly frightened, increasingly hungry, and still struggling to understand why the guards did not know he was the one who had tipped them off.

The guards sent him back to his cell.

On what seemed to be the morning of the third day, one of his interrogators and three other guards entered Shin's cell. They shackled his ankles, tied a rope to a hook in the ceiling, and hung him upside down. Then they left and locked the door—all without a word.

His feet almost touched the ceiling. His head was suspended about two feet above the floor. Reaching out with his hands, which the guards had left untied, Shin could not quite touch the floor. He squirmed and swung around trying to right himself, but could not. His neck cramped and his ankles hurt. Eventually his legs went numb. His head, flushed with blood, ached more with each hour.

Guards did not return until evening. They untied the boy and left, again without a word. Food arrived in his cell, but Shin found it almost impossible to eat. He could not move his fingers. His ankles, owing to the sharp steel edges of the shackles, were gouged and bleeding.

On the fourth day, the interrogators wore civilian clothes, not uniforms.

After being blindfolded and marched from his cell, Shin met them in a dimly lighted room with a high ceiling. It had the look of a machine shop.

A chain dangled from a winch on the ceiling. Hooks on the walls held a hammer, ax, pliers, and clubs of various shapes and sizes. On a wide shop table, Shin saw a large pair of pincers, a tool used for gripping and carrying pieces of hot metal.

"How is it, being in this room?" one of the interrogators asked.

Shin did not know what to say.

"I'll ask you just one more time," the chief interrogator said. "What were your father, mother, and brother planning to do after their escape?"

"I really don't know," Shin replied.

"If you tell the truth right now, I'll save you. If not, I'll kill you. Understand?"

Shin remembers paralyzing confusion.

"I've been easy on you until now because you are a kid," the interrogator said. "Don't try my patience."

Again, Shin failed to reply.

"This son of a bitch won't do!" the chief interrogator shouted.

The chief's lieutenants surrounded Shin and pulled off his clothes. Shackles were locked around his ankles and tied to the chain that hung from the ceiling. The winch started up, pulling Shin off his feet. His head hit the floor with a thud. His hands were bound together with a rope that was threaded through a hook on the ceiling. When the trussing was done, his body formed a U, his face and feet toward the ceiling, his bare back toward the floor.

The chief interrogator shouted more questions. Shin remembers giving no coherent answers. The chief told one of his men to fetch something.

A tub full of burning charcoal was dragged beneath Shin. One of the interrogators used a bellows to stoke the coals. The winch lowered Shin toward the flames.

"Keep going until he talks," the chief said.

Shin, crazed with pain, smelling his burning flesh, twisted away from the heat. One of the guards grabbed a gaff hook from the wall and pierced the boy in the lower abdomen, holding him over the fire until he lost consciousness.

He awoke in his cell. Guards had dressed him in his ill-fitting prison outfit, which he'd soiled with excrement and urine. He had no idea how long he had lain unconscious on the floor. His lower back was blistered and sticky with discharge. The flesh around his ankles had been scraped away.

For two days, Shin managed to crawl around in his cell and to eat.

Guards brought him whole steamed ears of corn, along with corn porridge and cabbage soup. But as his burns became infected, he grew feverish, lost his appetite, and found it nearly impossible to move.

Seeing Shin curled up on the floor of his cell, a guard shouted in the prison hallway, "That little runt is really tough."

Shin guesses ten days came and went before his final interrogation. It took place in his cell because he was too weak to get up off the floor. But he was no longer afraid. For the first time, he found words to defend himself.

"I was the one who reported this," he said. "I did a good job."

His interrogators didn't believe him. But instead of threatening or hurting Shin, they asked questions. He explained all that he had heard in his mother's house and what he had said to the night guard at school. He begged his interrogators to talk to Hong Sung Jo, the classmate who could confirm the story.

They promised nothing and left his cell.

Shin's fever grew worse. Blisters on his back swelled with pus. His cell smelled so bad that guards refused to step inside.

After several days (though the exact amount of time is unclear, as Shin was drifting in and out of delirium), guards opened his cell door and ordered two prisoners to go in. They picked him up and carried him down the corridor to another cell. Guards locked Shin inside. There was another prisoner in the cell.

Shin had been granted a reprieve. Hong had confirmed his story. Shin would never see the school's night guard again.

CHAPTER 7

THE SUN SHINES EVEN ON MOUSE HOLES

By the standards of Camp 14, Shin's cellmate was notably old, somewhere around fifty. He refused to explain why he was locked up in the camp's underground prison, but he did say he had been there for many years and that he sorely missed the sun.

Pallid, leathery skin sagged over his fleshless bones. His name was Kim Jin Myung. He asked to be called "Uncle."

Shin was in no condition to say much of anything for several weeks. Fever kept him curled up on the cold floor, where he expected to die. He could not eat and told his cellmate to take his food. Uncle ate some of it, but only until the boy's appetite returned.

In the meantime, Uncle went to work as Shin's full-time nurse.

He turned mealtimes into thrice-daily medical treatments, using a wooden spoon as a squeegee on Shin's infected blisters.

"There's a lot of pus here," he told Shin. "I'm going to scrape it away, so bear with me."

He rubbed salty cabbage soup into the wounds as a disinfectant. He massaged Shin's arms and legs so that his muscles would not atrophy. To prevent urine and feces from coming into contact with the boy's wounds, he carried the cell's chamber pot to Shin and hoisted him up so he could use it.

Shin guesses that this intensive care went on for about two months. He had a sense that Uncle had done this kind of work before, judging from his competence and calm.

On occasion, Shin and Uncle could hear the screams and moans of a prisoner being tortured. The room with the winch and the clubs seemed to be just down the corridor. Prison rules banned inmates from talking. But in their cell, which was just large enough for Shin and Uncle to lie side by side, they could whisper. Shin discovered later that guards knew about these conversations.

Uncle seemed to Shin to have special standing with the guards. They cut his hair and lent him scissors so he could trim his beard. They brought him cups of water. They told him the time of day when he asked. They gave him extra food, much of which he shared with Shin.

"Kid, you have a lot of days to live," Uncle said. "They say the sun shines even on mouse holes."

The old man's medical skills and his caring words kept the boy alive. His fever waned, his mind cleared, and his burns congealed into scars.

It was Shin's first exposure to sustained kindness, and he was grateful beyond words. But he also found it puzzling. He had not trusted his mother to keep him from starving. At school, he trusted no one, with the possible exception of Hong Sung Jo, and informed on everyone. In return, he expected abuse and betrayal. In the cell, Uncle slowly reconfigured those expectations. The old man said he was lonely and seemed genuinely happy to share his space and his meals with someone else. He never once angered or frightened Shin or undermined his recovery.

The routines of prison life following Shin's interrogation and torture—discounting the screaming that periodically echoed down the prison corridor—were oddly sustaining.

Although the food was tasteless, guards delivered enough of it for Shin and Uncle to survive. There was no dangerous outside labor, no exhausting work quotas. For the first time in his life, Shin wasn't expected to do any physical labor.

Other than nursing the boy, Uncle was a man of leisure. He exercised daily in his cell. He cut Shin's hair. He was an entertaining talker, whose knowledge of North Korea thrilled Shin, especially when the subject was food.

"Uncle, tell me a story," Shin would say.

The old man described what food outside the fence looked, smelled, and tasted like. Thanks to his loving descriptions of roasting pork, boiling chicken, and eating clams at the seashore, Shin's appetite came back with a vengeance.

As his health improved, guards began to call him out of the cell. They were now very much aware that Shin had snitched on his own family. They pressed him to inform on the old man.

"You two are in there together," a guard said to Shin. "What does he say? Don't conceal anything."

Back in the cell, Uncle wanted to know, "What did they ask you?"

Squeezed between his nurse and his jailers, Shin elected to tell the truth to both sides. He told Uncle that the guards had asked him to be an informer. This did not surprise the old man. He continued to entertain Shin with long stories about good things to eat. But he did not volunteer biographical information. He would not talk about his family. He expressed no opinions about the government.

Shin guessed—based on the way Uncle used language—that he had once been an important and well-educated man. But it was only a guess.

Although it was a crime to talk about escaping from Camp 14, it was not against the rules to fantasize about what life would be like if the government were to set you free. Uncle told Shin that both of them would one day be released. Until then, he said, they had a sacred obligation to stay strong, live as long as possible, and never consider suicide.

"What do you think?" Uncle would then ask Shin. "Do you believe I'll also be able to make it out?"

Shin doubted it, but said nothing.

A guard unlocked the door of Shin's cell and handed him the school uniform he had worn on the day he arrived in the underground prison.

"Put on these clothes and come along quickly," the guard said.

As Shin changed, he asked Uncle what would happen. The old man assured him that he would be safe and that they would meet again on the outside.

"Let me hold you once," he said, grasping both of Shin's hands tightly.

Shin did not want to leave the cell. He had never trusted—never loved—anyone before. In the years ahead, he would think of the old man in the dark room far more often and with far greater affection than he thought of his parents. But after guards led him out of the cell and locked its door, he never saw Uncle again.

CHAPTER 8

AVOIDING MOTHER'S EYES

They took Shin to the big bare room where, in early April, he had first been interrogated. Now, it was late November. Shin had just turned fourteen. He had not seen the sun for more than half a year.

What he did see in the room startled him: his father knelt in front of two interrogators who sat at their desks. He seemed much older and more careworn than before. He had been brought into the underground prison at about the same time as Shin.

Kneeling beside him, Shin saw that his father's right leg canted outward in an unnatural way. Shin Gyung Sub had also been tortured. Below his knee, his leg bones had been broken, and they had knitted back together at an odd angle. The injury would end his relatively comfortable job as a camp mechanic and lathe operator. He would now have to hobble around as an unskilled laborer on a construction crew.

During his time in the underground prison, guards told Shin's father that his youngest son had informed them of the escape plan. When Shin later had a chance to talk to his father about this, the conversation was strained. His father said it was better to have told the guards than to have risked concealing the plan. But his caustic tone confused Shin. He sounded as if he knew his son's first instinct was to inform.

"Read it and stamp it," one of the interrogators said, handing a document to Shin and one to his father.

It was a nondisclosure form stipulating that father and son would not tell anyone what had gone on inside the prison. If they did talk, the document said, they would be punished.

After pressing their inked thumbs to their respective forms, they were handcuffed, blindfolded, and led outside to the elevator. Above ground, their cuffs and blindfolds still on, they were guided into the backseat of a small car and driven away.

In the car, Shin guessed that he and his father would be released back into the camp's population. Guards would not force them to sign a secrecy pledge and then shoot them. It did not make sense. But when the car stopped after about thirty minutes and his blindfold was removed, he panicked.

A crowd had gathered at the empty wheat field near his mother's house. This was the place where Shin had witnessed two or three executions a year since he was a toddler. A makeshift gallows had been constructed and a wooden pole had been driven into the ground.

Shin was now certain that he and his father were to be executed. He became acutely aware of the air passing into and out of his lungs. He told himself these were the last breaths of his life.

His panic subsided when a guard barked out his father's name.

"Hey, Gyung Sub. Go sit at the very front."

Shin was told to go with his father. A guard removed their handcuffs. They sat down. The officer overseeing the execution began to speak. Shin's mother and brother were dragged out.

Shin had not seen them or heard anything about their fate since he walked out of his mother's house on the night he betrayed them.

"Execute Jang Hye Gyung and Shin He Geun, traitors of the people," the senior officer said.

Shin looked at his father. He was weeping silently.

The shame Shin feels about the executions has been compounded over the years by the lies he began telling in South Korea.

"There is nothing in my life to compare with this burden," Shin told me on the day in California when he explained how and why he had misrepresented his past.

But he was not ashamed on the day of the executions. He was angry. He hated his mother and brother with the savage clarity of a wronged and wounded adolescent.

As he saw it, he had been tortured and nearly died, and his father had been crippled, because of their foolish, self-centered scheming.

And only minutes before he saw them on the execution grounds, Shin had believed he would be shot because of their recklessness.

When guards dragged her to the gallows, Shin saw that his mother looked bloated. They forced her to stand on a wooden box, gagged her, tied her arms behind her back, and tightened a noose around her neck. They did not cover her swollen eyes.

She scanned the crowd and found Shin. He refused to hold her gaze.

When guards pulled away the box, she jerked about desperately. As he watched his mother struggle, Shin thought she deserved to die.

Shin's brother looked gaunt and frail as guards tied him to the wooden post. Three guards fired their rifles three times. Bullets snapped the rope that held his forehead to the pole. It was a bloody, brain-splattered mess of a killing, a spectacle that sickened and frightened Shin. But he thought his brother, too, had deserved it.

CHAPTER 9

REACTIONARY SON OF A BITCH

Executions of parents for attempted escape were not uncommon in Camp 14. Shin witnessed several before and after his mother's hanging. It wasn't clear, though, what happened to the children they left behind in the camp. As far as Shin could determine, none of these children were allowed to go to school.

Except for him.

Perhaps because he was a proven snitch, camp authorities sent him back to school. But his return wasn't easy.

Trouble started as soon as Shin walked from the execution grounds to his school, where he had a private meeting with his teacher. Shin had known this man for two years (although he never learned his name) and regarded him as relatively fair-minded, at least by camp standards.

At the meeting, though, the teacher was seething. He wanted to know why Shin had tipped off the school's night guard about the escape plot.

"Why didn't you come to me first?" he shouted.

"I wanted to, but I couldn't find you," Shin replied, explaining that it was late at night and the teachers' compound was off-limits to prisoners.

"You could have waited until the morning," the teacher said.

The teacher had not received any credit from his superiors for uncovering the escape plot. He blamed this miscarriage of justice on Shin and warned the boy that he would pay for his thoughtlessness. When Shin's class, about thirty-five students, assembled later in the classroom, the teacher pointed at Shin and shouted, "Come up front. Kneel!"

Shin knelt on the concrete floor for nearly six hours. When he wiggled to ease his discomfort, the teacher whacked him with a blackboard pointer.

On his second day back at school, Shin walked with his class to a camp farm to gather corn straw and haul it to a threshing floor. Shin pulled an A-frame carrier loaded with straw. It was relatively light work compared to pushing coal carts, but it required that he wear a kind of harness with a leather strap that chafed the tender scars on his lower back and tailbone.

Soon, blood was oozing down his legs. The pants of his school uniform were soaked.

Shin dared not complain. His teacher had warned him that he would need to work harder than his classmates to wash away the sins of his mother and brother.

At school and during field work, all students had to ask permission to urinate or defecate. When Shin made his first bathroom request after his release from prison, his teacher said no. Shin tried to hold it during the school day, but ended up peeing his pants a couple of times a week, usually when he and other students were working outside. Since it was winter and very cold, he worked in pants stiff with urine.

Shin had known most of his classmates since they were seven years old and started primary school together. He was smaller than most of the boys in his class, but they had usually treated him as a peer. Now, taking their cue from the teacher, they began to taunt and bully him.

They snatched away his food, punched him in the stomach, and called him names. Almost all the names were elaborations on "reactionary son of a bitch."

Shin is not certain whether his classmates knew he had betrayed his mother and brother. He believes that his childhood friend, Hong, did not tell anyone. In any case, Shin was never teased for having betrayed his family. That would have been an unpatriotic and risky schoolyard taunt, since all students were under orders from teachers and guards to inform on their families and on each other.

Before his time in prison, Shin had managed to make a strategic classroom alliance. He had become friends with Hong Joo Hyun, the grade leader. (This was the job Shin had tried to win on the night he snitched on his family.) Hong led students on work details and was authorized by the teacher to hit and kick classmates he regarded as shirkers. He was also the teacher's most trusted informer.

Hong himself could be beaten or denied meals if the class dithered during field work and failed to meet quotas. His position was similar to adult prisoners known as *jagubbanang*, or crew managers. Guards gave these managers, who were always male and tended to be physically imposing, virtually unchecked authority over their fellow prisoners. Since the managers had to answer for any failures by their crews, they were often more vigilant, brutal, and unforgiving than camp guards.

After Shin's mother and brother were executed, Hong began to watch Shin carefully. During a road repair assignment, he noticed that Shin had loaded far too many stones in a handcart. Shin tried again and again to push the cart, but it was too heavy for the emaciated boy to budge.

When Shin saw his grade leader approaching with a shovel, he initially expected some help. He thought that Hong would order other students to pitch in and roll the cart. Instead, Hong swung his shovel and struck Shin in the back, knocking him to the ground.

"Pull your handcart correctly," Hong said.

He kicked Shin in the side of the head and told him to stand up. As Shin struggled to get to his feet, Hong again swung his shovel and mashed Shin's nose, which began to bleed.

After that beating, students who were younger and smaller than Shin began to insult his mother. With the encouragement of the teacher, they called him names and punched him.

Owing to his confinement in the underground cell, Shin had lost much of his strength and nearly all of his endurance. His return to hard labor, long hours, and skimpy meals at school made him almost insanely hungry.

In the school cafeteria, he scrounged constantly for spilled cabbage soup, dipping his hand in cold dirty soup that had spilled on the floor and licking his fingers clean. He searched floors, roads, and fields for grains of rice, beans, or cow dung that contained undigested kernels of corn.

On a morning work detail in December, a couple of weeks after his return to school, Shin discovered a dried-up ear of corn in a pile of straw and devoured it. Hong Joo Hyun was nearby. He ran over to Shin, grabbed him by the hair, and dragged him to their nearby teacher.

"Teacher, instead of working, Shin is just scavenging for food."

As Shin fell to his knees to beg for forgiveness (a ritual abasement that he performed as a matter of instinct), his teacher hit him in the head with his walking stick and shouted for the rest of the class to help punish the scavenger.

"Come here and slap him," the teacher said.

Shin knew what was coming. He had slapped and punched many of his classmates in a round-robin of collective punishment. Students queued up in front of Shin. Girls slapped him on the right cheek, boys on the left. Shin believes they went through five rotations before the teacher said it was time for lunch.

Before his confinement in the secret prison and before his teacher and schoolmates began picking on him, Shin hadn't thought to blame anyone for his birth inside Camp 14.

His blinkered existence kept him focused on finding food and avoiding beatings. He was indifferent to the outside world, to his parents, and to the history of his family. As much as he believed in anything, he believed the guards' preaching about original sin. As the offspring of traitors, his one chance at redemption—and his only way of averting starvation—was hard work.

Back at school, however, he bristled with resentment. He was not yet hobbled by guilt about his mother and brother; that would come much later. But his months in the cell with Uncle had lifted, if only slightly, a curtain on the world beyond the fence.

Shin had become conscious of what he could never eat and never see. The filth, stink, and bleakness of the camp crushed his spirit. As he become marginally self-aware, he discovered loneliness, regret, and longing.

Most of all, he was angry with both his parents. His mother's scheming, he believed, had triggered his torture. He blamed her, too, for the abuse and humiliation dished out by his teacher and classmates. He despised both his mother and his father for selfishly breeding in a labor camp, for producing offspring doomed to die behind barbed wire.

Out on the execution grounds, in the moments after Shin's mother and brother were killed, Shin's father had tried to comfort the boy.

"You okay? Are you hurt anywhere? Did you see your mother in there?" his father asked repeatedly, referring to the underground prison.

Shin was too angry to reply.

After the execution, he even found it distasteful to say the word "father." On his rare days off from school—about fourteen days a year—Shin was expected to go see him. During the visits, Shin would often refuse to speak.

His father tried to apologize.

"I know you're suffering because you have the wrong parents," he told Shin. "You were unlucky to be born to us. What can you do? Things just turned out this way."

Suicide is a powerful temptation for North Koreans plucked out of ordinary lives and subjected to the labor camps' regime of hard labor, hunger, beatings, and sleep deprivation.

"Suicide was not uncommon in the camp," Kang Chol-hwan wrote in his memoir about the decade he spent inside Camp 15. "A number of our neighbors took that road . . . They usually left behind letters criticizing the regime, or at the very least its Security Force. . . . Truth be told, some form of punishment would await the family regardless of whether or not a critical note were left behind. It was a rule that admitted no exceptions. The Party saw suicide as an attempt to escape its grasp, and if the individual who had tried the trick wasn't around to pay for it, someone else needed to be found."[1]

North Korea's National Security Agency warns all prisoners that suicide will be punished with longer sentences for surviving relatives, according to the Korean Bar Association in Seoul.

In his memoir about six years in two of the camps, Kim Yong, a former lieutenant colonel in the North Korean army, says the appeal of suicide was "overwhelming."

"Prisoners were beyond the point of feeling hungry, so they felt constantly delirious," wrote Kim, who said he spent two years at Camp

14 until he was transferred across the Taedong River to Camp 18, a political prison where guards were less brutal and prisoners had slightly more freedom.

Trying to end the delirium he felt in Camp 14, Kim said he jumped down a coal mine shaft. After tumbling to the bottom of the mine, badly injured, he felt more disappointment than pain: "I regretted that I could not find a better way to really put an end to this indescribable torment."[2]

As wretched as Shin's life became after the execution of his mother and brother, suicide for him was never more than a passing thought.

There was a fundamental difference, in his view, between prisoners who arrived from the outside and those who were born in the camp: many outsiders, shattered by the contrast between a comfortable past and a punishing present, could not find or maintain the will to survive. A perverse benefit of birth in the camp was a complete absence of expectations.

And so Shin's misery never skidded into complete hopelessness. He had no hope to lose, no past to mourn, no pride to defend. He did not find it degrading to lick soup off the floor. He was not ashamed to beg a guard for forgiveness. It didn't trouble his conscience to betray a friend for food. These were merely survival skills, not motives for suicide.

Teachers at Shin's school rarely rotated to other jobs. In the seven years since he had entered school, he had known only two teachers. But four months after the execution, Shin caught a break. One morning, the teacher who tormented him—and who encouraged his classmates to do likewise—was gone.

His replacement gave no outward indications that he would be any less abusive. Like nearly every guard in the camp, he was a nameless, bullish-looking man in his early thirties who demanded that students avert their eyes and bow their heads when they spoke to him. Shin remembers him being just as cold, distant, and domineering as the others.

The new teacher, though, did not seem to want Shin to die of malnutrition.

By March 1997, about four months after his release from the underground prison, starvation had become a real possibility for Shin. Harassed by his teacher and fellow students, he could not find enough nourishment to maintain his weight. He could not seem to recover from his burns. His scars still bled. He grew weaker and often failed to complete his work assignments, which led to more beatings, less food, more bleeding.

The new teacher took Shin to the cafeteria after mealtimes. He told the boy to eat whatever leftovers he could find. He sometimes sneaked food to Shin. He also assigned him less arduous work and made certain that Shin had a warm place to sleep on the floor of the student dormitory.

As important, the new teacher prevented Shin's classmates from hitting him and stealing his food. The taunting about his dead mother ended. Hong Joo Hyun, the class leader who had struck him in the face with a shovel, again became his friend. Shin put on some weight. The burns on his back finally healed.

Perhaps the teacher felt pity for a picked-on child who had watched his mother die. It is also possible that senior guards in the camp had found out that a disgruntled teacher was mistreating a reliable snitch. Perhaps the replacement teacher was ordered to keep the boy alive.

Why the new teacher made the effort, Shin never had a clue. But Shin is certain that without his help, he would have died.

CHAPTER 10
WORKING MAN

Tractors hauled food to the work site every day. There were heaps of milled corn and steaming vats of cabbage soup.

Shin was fifteen and working alongside thousands of prisoners. It was 1998 and they were building a hydroelectric dam on the Taedong River, which forms the southern border of Camp 14. The project was urgent enough to warrant filling the stomachs of slave laborers three times a day. Guards also allowed workers—about five thousand adult prisoners and a couple of hundred students from the camp's secondary school—to catch fish and frogs from the river.

For the first time in his life, Shin ate well for an entire year.

The North Korean government had decided that the camp, with its high-voltage fence and factories that churned out military uniforms, glassware, and cement, needed a reliable local source of electricity, and fast.

"Hey! Hey! Hey! It's falling! Falling!"

Shin shouted the warning. He was hauling platters of wet concrete to the crew when he noticed that a freshly poured concrete wall had cracked and was beginning to collapse. Beneath it, a crew of eight was finishing another wall.

He screamed as loudly as he could. But it was too late.

All the workers—three adults, along with three fifteen-year-old girls and two fifteen-year-old boys—were killed. Several were crushed beyond recognition. The supervising guard did not halt work after the accident. At the end of the shift, he simply ordered Shin and other workers to dispose of the bodies.

The mountains of North Korea are crisscrossed with swift rivers, large and small. Their hydropower potential is such that ninety percent of the electricity on the Korean Peninsula prior to partition came from the North.[1]

But under the Kim family dynasty, the North Korean government has failed to build or maintain a reliable national electricity grid linked to hydroelectric dams, many of which are located in remote areas. When the Soviet Union stopped supplying cheap fuel oil in the early 1990s, city-based, oil-powered generators sputtered to a halt. The lights went out across much of the country. Most of the time, they are still out.

Satellite photographs of the Korean Peninsula at night show a black hole between China and South Korea. There is not enough power in the country even to keep the lights on in Pyongyang, where the government tries to pamper the elite. In February 2008, when I traveled for three days and two nights to Pyongyang as part of a large delegation of foreign journalists to cover a performance by the New York Philharmonic, the government managed to turn on the lights in much of the city. When the orchestra and the press left town, the lights went out again.

It makes sense, then, that the construction of small and medium-sized hydroelectric plants—capable of serving local industry and built mostly by hand, using basic technology—has been a priority since the 1990s. In a frenzy of hard labor, thousands have been built.

Besides staving off economic collapse, the dams are ideologically beguiling to the family that runs the country. As his hagiographers tell the story, Kim Il Sung's most important intellectual achievement—his brilliant *juche* idea—asserts that national pride goes hand in glove with self-reliance.

As the Great Leader explained it:

> Establishing *juche* means, in a nutshell,
> being the master of revolution and
> reconstruction in one's own country. This
> means holding fast to an independent
> position, rejecting dependence on others,
> using one's own brains, believing in
> one's own strength, displaying the
> revolutionary spirit of self-reliance, and
> thus solving one's own problems for
> oneself on one's own responsibility under
> all circumstances.[2]

None of this, of course, is even remotely possible in a country as ill governed as North Korea. It has always depended on handouts from foreign governments, and if they end, the Kim dynasty would probably collapse. Even in the best of years, it cannot feed itself. North Korea has no oil, and its economy has never been able to generate enough cash to buy sufficient fuel or food on the world market.

North Korea would have lost the Korean War and disappeared as a state without the help of the Chinese, who fought the United States and other Western forces to a stalemate. Until the 1990s, North Korea's economy was largely held together by subsidies from the Soviet Union. From 2000 to 2008, South Korea propped up the North—and bought itself a measure of peaceful coexistence—with huge unconditional gifts of fertilizer and food, along with generous investment.

Since then, Pyongyang has become increasingly dependent on China for concessional trade, food aid, and fuel. A telling measure of China's growing influence is that in the months prior to Kim Jong Eun's official emergence in 2010 as the chosen successor to Kim Jong Il, the ailing elder Kim traveled twice to Beijing, where diplomats say he asked for China to bless his succession plan.

Reality notwithstanding, North Korea champions self-reliance as the sine qua non of the country's much-advertised goal of becoming "a great, prosperous and powerful nation" by 2012, the one-hundredth anniversary of the birth of Kim Il Sung.

To that fantastical end, the government regularly enlists the masses in miserable tasks dressed up in noble slogans. The propaganda can be quite creative: the famine was repackaged as the "Arduous March," a patriotic struggle that North Koreans were encouraged to win with the inspiring slogan: "Let's Eat Two Meals Per Day."

In the spring of 2010, as food shortages again became severe, the government launched a massive back-to-the-farm campaign to persuade city dwellers to move to the countryside and raise crops. These urbanites were to be permanent reinforcements for "rice-planting combat," the annual campaign that sends office workers, students, and soldiers to the countryside for two months in the spring and two weeks in the fall. In the winter, city people are charged with collecting their feces (and that of their neighbors) for spring planting.

Other urgent and patriotic tasks that North Koreans have been urged to shoulder include "Let's Breed More High-Yielding Fish!," "Let's Expand Goat Rearing and Create More Grassland in Accordance with the Party!," and "Let's Grow More Sunflowers!" The success of these hortatory campaigns has been mixed, at best, especially when it comes to the government's highly unpopular efforts to lure city-bred people into back-breaking farm labor.

For the dam project inside Camp 14, there were no such problems with motivation.

As Shin witnessed it, soon after guards announced a new "rally of endeavor" to build a hydroelectric dam, thousands of adult prisoners marched from factories to makeshift dormitories erected near the north bank of the Taedong. Shin and his classmates moved out of their school dormitory. They all worked, ate, and slept at the dam site, located about six miles southeast of the center of the camp.

Labor on the dam—which satellite photographs show to be a substantial concrete structure spanning a wide river, with turbines and spillways hugging the northern bank—went on around the clock. Trucks hauled in cement, sand, and rock. Shin saw only one diesel-powered excavator. Most of the digging and construction was done by workers using shovels, buckets, and bare hands.

Shin had seen prisoners die in the camp before—of hunger, illness, beatings, and at public executions—but not as a routine part of work.

The greatest loss of life at the dam occurred soon after full-scale construction began. A rainy season flash flood rolled down the Taedong in July 1998, sweeping away hundreds of dam workers and students. Shin watched them disappear from a perch on the riverbank where he was hauling sand. He was quickly put to work confirming the identities of dead students and burying their bodies.

On the third day after the flood, he remembers carrying the bloated body of a girl on his back. At first it was slack, but it soon became stiff, with rigid arms and legs splayed outward. To squeeze the body into a narrow, hand-dug grave, he had to push the limbs together.

Floodwaters stripped some drowned students of their clothes.

When Hong Joo Hyun discovered a naked classmate amid the post-flood debris, he removed his own clothes and covered the body.

As the cleanup continued, Shin competed with many other students to find bodies. For each corpse they buried, guards rewarded them with one or two servings of rice.

The Taedong, as it flowed past Camp 14, was too wide and swift to freeze in the North Korean winter, which allowed dam construction to continue year round. In December 1998, Shin was ordered to wade into the river's shallows to pick up boulders. Unable to bear the cold and without the approval of his guard, he joined several other students who tried to wade out.

"You come out of the water and I'll starve you all, understand!" their guard shouted.

Shivering uncontrollably, Shin kept working.

Students worked primarily as bottom-rung laborers. They often carried steel reinforcing rods to older workmen who tied them together with twine or wire as the dam rose from the riverbed in a checkerboard pattern of concrete blocks. None of the students had gloves, and in winter their hands sometimes stuck to the cold rods. Handing over a rebar sometimes meant ripping skin from one's palms and fingers.

Shin remembers that when one of his classmates, Byun Soon Ho, complained about a fever and feeling unwell, a guard gave him a lesson in the benefits of stoicism.

"Soon Ho, stick out your tongue," the guard said.

He ordered the boy to press his tongue to a freezing rebar. Nearly an hour later, Soon Ho, tears in his eyes, his mouth oozing blood, managed to detach his tongue.

Working at the dam was dangerous, but Shin also found it exhilarating.

The primary reason was food. It was not particularly tasty, but month in and month out there was lots of it. Shin remembers mealtimes at the dam site as the happiest moments of his teen years. He regained all the weight and stamina he had lost in the underground prison. He could keep up at work. He became confident in his ability to survive.

Living near the dam also gave Shin a small measure of independence. In the summer, hundreds of students slept outdoors under a canopy. When they were not working, they could walk—during daylight hours—anywhere inside the sprawl of Camp 14. For his hard work, Shin earned a recommendation from his grade leader that allowed him to leave the dam site for four overnight visits to his father. Since they were not reconciled, Shin spent just one night with him.

He had worked at the dam for about a year when his time at secondary school came to an end in May 1999. The school had been little more than slave quarters from which he was sent out as a rock picker, weed puller, and dam laborer. But graduation meant that, at age sixteen, he had become an adult worker. He was ready to be assigned to a permanent job inside the camp.

About sixty percent of Shin's class was assigned to the coal mines, where accidental death from cave-ins, explosions, and gas poisonings was common. Many miners developed black lung disease after ten to fifteen years of working underground. Most miners died in their forties, if not before. As Shin understood it, an assignment in the mines was a death sentence.

The decision about who went where was made by Shin's teacher, the man who two years earlier had saved Shin's life by providing him with extra food and halting abuse from his classmates. The teacher handed down assignments without explanation, curtly telling students where they would spend the rest of their lives. As soon as the teacher made his announcements, new masters—foremen from camp factories, mines, and farms—came to the school and led students away.

The teacher told Hong Joo Hyun that he was going to the mines. Shin never saw him again.

The girl who lost her big toe in the mines at the age of eleven, Moon Sung Sim, was assigned to the textile factory.

Hong Sung Jo, the friend who saved Shin from his torturers by confirming that he'd informed on his mother and brother, was also sent to the mines. Shin never saw him again, either.

If there was a rationale behind the assignments, Shin never understood it. He thinks it came down to the personal whim of the teacher, who was consistently unreadable. Perhaps the teacher liked Shin. Perhaps he pitied him. Maybe he had been ordered to look out for the boy. Shin just doesn't know.

In any case, the teacher again saved his life. He assigned him to a permanent job at Camp 14's pig farm, where two hundred men and women raised about eight hundred pigs, along with goats, rabbits, chickens, and a few cows. Feed for the animals was grown in fields surrounding the livestock pens.

"Shin In Geun, you're assigned to the ranch," the teacher told him. "Work hard."

Nowhere else in Camp 14 was there so much food to steal.

CHAPTER 11

NAPPING ON THE FARM

Shin did not work hard.

The foremen would sometimes beat him and other workers who performed poorly, but not seriously and never to death. The pig farm was as good as it got for Shin at Camp 14. He even sneaked the occasional midafternoon nap.

Mealtime portions in the farm's cafeteria were no larger than at the cement factory, the textile mill, or the mines. Nor was the food any better. But between meals, Shin could help himself to ground corn intended for the piglets he fed between November and July. Out in the fields, where he weeded and harvested from August to October, he snacked on corn, cabbage, and other vegetables. On occasion, the foremen would bring a cooking pot out to the fields and everyone could eat his or her fill.

The farm was located up in the hills, away from the river, about a half hour's walk from Shin's former school and the house where he had lived with his mother. Women with children walked back and forth to the farm from family housing, but most of the farmworkers stayed in a dormitory on the farm.

Shin slept there on the floor in a room for men. Bullying was not a problem. He did not have to fight for a warm patch of concrete. He slept well.

There was a slaughterhouse on the farm where fifty or so pigs were butchered twice a year, exclusively for guards and their families. As a prisoner, Shin was not allowed to eat pork or the meat of any livestock raised on the farm. But he and other prisoners could sometimes steal. The smell of roasting pork on the farm would alert guards, leading to beatings and weeks of half rations, so they ate purloined pork raw.

What Shin did not do on the farm was think, talk, or dream about the outside world.

No one there mentioned the escape plan that had led to the execution of his mother and brother. Guards did not ask Shin to snitch on fellow workers. The anger that overwhelmed him in the wake of his mother's death receded into numbness. Before he was tortured, confined in the underground prison, and exposed to Uncle's stories about the world beyond the fence, Shin had been uninterested in anything beyond his next meal.

On the pig farm, that passive blankness returned. Shin uses the word "relaxing" to describe his time on the camp farm, which lasted from 1999 to 2003.

Outside the camp during those years, life in North Korea was anything but relaxing.

Famine and floods in the mid-1990s all but destroyed the centrally planned economy. The government's Public Distribution System, which had fed most North Koreans since the 1950s, collapsed. As a panicked response to hunger and starvation, barter trade ran wild and private markets exploded in number and importance. Nine out of ten households traded to survive.[1] More and more North Koreans sneaked across the border into China for food, work, trade, and flight to South

Korea. Neither China nor North Korea released figures, but estimates of these economic migrants ranged from tens of thousands to four hundred thousand.

Kim Jong Il tried to control the chaos. His government created a new network of detention centers for traders who traveled without authorization. But with crackers and cigarettes they could often buy their freedom from hungry police and soldiers. Rail stations, open-air markets, and back alleys in major towns became crowded with starving drifters. The many orphaned children found in these places became known as "wandering sparrows."

Shin did not yet know this, but grassroots capitalism, vagabond trading, and rampant corruption were creating cracks in the police state that surrounded Camp 14.

Food aid from the United States, Japan, South Korea, and other donors mitigated the worst of the famine by the late 1990s. But in an indirect and accidental way, it also energized the market ladies and traveling entrepreneurs who would give Shin sustenance, cover, and guidance in his escape to China.

Unlike any other aid recipient in the world, North Korea's government insisted on sole authority for transporting donated food. The demand angered the United States, the largest aid donor, and it frustrated the monitoring techniques that the U.N. World Food Program had developed around the world to track aid and make sure it reached intended recipients. But since the need was so urgent and the death toll so high, the West swallowed its disgust and delivered more than one billion dollars' worth of food to North Korea between 1995 and 2003.

During these years, refugees from North Korea arrived in the South and told government officials that they had seen donated rice, wheat, corn, vegetable oil, nonfat dry milk, fertilizer, medicine, winter clothing, blankets, bicycles, and other aid items on sale in private markets. Pictures and videos taken in the markets showed bags of grain marked as "A Gift from the American People."

Bureaucrats, party officials, army officers, and other well-placed government elites ended up stealing about thirty percent of the aid, according to estimates by outside scholars and international aid agencies. They sold it to private traders, often for dollars or euros, and delivered the goods using government vehicles.

Without intending to do so, wealthy donor countries injected a kind of adrenaline rush into the grubby world of North Korean street trading. The lucrative theft of international food aid whetted the appetite of higher-ups for easy money as it helped transform private markets into the country's primary economic engine.

Private markets, which today supply most of the food North Koreans eat, have become the fundamental reason why most outside experts say a catastrophic 1990s-style famine is unlikely to happen again.

The markets, though, have not come close to eliminating hunger or malnutrition. They also appear to have increased inequity, creating a chasm between those who have figured out how to trade and those who have not.

In late 1998, a few months before Shin was assigned to the pig farm, the World Food Program conducted a nutrition survey of children, which covered seventy percent of North Korea. It found that about two thirds of those surveyed were stunted or underweight. The numbers were double that of Angola, then at the end of a long civil war, and the North Korean government became furious when they were released to the public.

Ten years later, when private markets in the North were well established and selling everything from imported fruit to Chinese-made CD players, nutrition in state-run institutions for children and the elderly had barely improved, according to a World Food Program nutrition survey that was tolerated by the government as a condition of receiving aid.

"The children looked very sad, very emaciated, very pathetic," a nutritionist who worked on the 2008 food survey told me. She had participated in previous nutrition surveys dating back to the late 1990s and concluded that chronic hunger and severe malnutrition had persisted in much of North Korea despite the spread of markets.

International nutrition surveys have also found a pervasive pattern of geographic inequity. Hunger, stunting, and wasting diseases are three to four times more prevalent in remote provinces of North Korea—home to the hostile classes—than they are in and around Pyongyang.

As Shin found in the labor camp, the most secure place for powerless North Koreans to live amid chronic hunger is a farm. By all indications, farmers (excepting those whose land was ruined by floods) weathered the famine far better than city dwellers. Even though they worked on cooperative farms, where crops belonged to the state, they were in a position to hide and hoard food, as well as to sell it for cash or trade it for clothing and other necessities.

The government had little choice—after the famine, after the collapse of its food distribution system, and after the rise of the private markets—but to offer farmers higher prices and increase incentives to grow more food. Private farming on small plots of land was legalized in 2002. This allowed more private farm-to-market trade, which increased the power of traders and the autonomy of productive farmers.

Kim Jong Il, however, never warmed to market reform. His government called it "honey-coated poison."

"It is important to decisively frustrate capitalist and non-socialist elements in their bud," according to the *Rodong Sinmun*, the party newspaper in Pyongyang. "Once the imperialist ideological and cultural poisoning is tolerated, even the faith unshakable before the threat of a bayonet will be bound to give in like a wet mud-wall."

The capitalism that bloomed in the cities and small towns of North Korea weakened the government's iron grip on everyday life and did little to enrich the state. Kim Jong Il grumbled publicly, saying, "Frankly the state has no money, but individuals have two years' budget worth."[2]

His government counterattacked.

As part of the "military first" era that Kim's government officially proclaimed in 1999, the Korean People's Army, with more than a million soldiers to feed three times a day, moved aggressively to confiscate a substantial slice of all food grown on cooperative farms.

"At harvest time, soldiers bring their own trucks to the farms and just take," Kwon Tae-jin, a specialist on North Korean agriculture at the Korea Rural Economic Institute, which is funded by the South Korean government, told me in Seoul.

In the far north, where food supplies are historically lean and farmers are regarded as politically hostile, the military takes a quarter of total grain production, Kwon said. In other areas of the country, it takes five to seven percent. To make sure that workers at state farms do not shortchange the military, the army stations soldiers at all three thousand of them throughout the harvest season. When tens of thousands of city dwellers are brought to the farms to assist with the fall harvest, soldiers monitor them to make sure they do not steal food.

The permanent deployment of soldiers on farms has spawned corruption. Kwon said that farm managers pay off soldiers, who then turn a blind eye to large-scale theft of food that is later sold in private markets. Disputes among groups of corrupt soldiers periodically lead to fistfights and shootouts, according to a number of defectors and reports by aid groups. Good Friends, the Buddhist aid group with informants in the North, reported in 2009 that one soldier on a state farm was stabbed with a sickle during a fight over corn.

Sealed away on the pig farm, Shin heard nothing about the street trading, corruption, and extralegal intercity travel that would—in less than two years' time—help him escape.

Holed up on a mountaintop that was a kind of camp within the camp, he drifted uneventfully through the last of his teenage years, keeping his head down, his mind blank, and his energies focused on stealing food. His most vivid memory of those years was getting busted for barbecuing stolen pig intestines. He was beaten, deprived of food for five days, and his cafeteria rations were cut in half for three months.

Turning twenty on the farm, he believed he had found the place where he would grow old and die.

But the pig farm interlude ended abruptly in March 2003. For reasons never explained, Shin was transferred to the camp's garment factory, a crowded, chaotic, stressful work site where two thousand women and five hundred men made military uniforms.

At the factory, Shin's life again became complicated. There was relentless pressure to meet production quotas. There was renewed pressure to snitch. Guards scavenged for sex among the factory's seamstresses.

There was also a newcomer, an educated prisoner from Pyongyang. He had been schooled in Europe and had lived in China. He was to tell Shin about what he was missing.

CHAPTER 12

SEWING AND SNITCHING

A thousand women stitched together military uniforms during twelve-hour shifts. When their temperamental foot-powered sewing machines broke down, Shin fixed them.

He was responsible for about fifty machines and the seamstresses who operated them. If the machines did not spew out their daily quota of army uniforms, Shin and the seamstresses were forced to perform "bitter humiliation work," which meant two extra hours on the floor of the factory, usually from ten to midnight.

Experienced seamstresses could keep their machines in working order, but those who were new, inept, or very ill could not. To fix a broken machine, which was forged out of cast iron at a foundry inside Camp 14, Shin and other repairmen had to haul it on their backs to a repair shop upstairs.

The extra labor incensed many of the repairmen, who took their anger out on seamstresses by grabbing their hair, slamming their heads against walls, and kicking them in the face. Foremen in the factory, who were prisoners chosen by guards for their toughness, generally looked the other way when seamstresses were beaten. They told Shin that fear encouraged production.

Although he was still short and skinny, Shin was no longer a passive, malnourished, and torture-traumatized child. During his first year in the factory, he proved it to himself and to his coworkers in a confrontation with another sewing machine repairman.

Gong Jin Soo was a hot head. Shin had watched him go into a rage when one of the seamstresses in Gong's stable broke the axle of a sewing machine. Gong kicked the woman in the face until she collapsed to the floor.

When Gong demanded a feed dog—a crucial part of a sewing machine that controls stitch size by regulating the speed of fabric moving to the needle—from a seamstress who worked with Shin, she curtly refused.

"Bitch, if a repairman asks you for a part, you give it," Gong said. "What are you looking at with your eyes all raised?"

As Shin watched, Gong punched her in the face and bloodied her nose.

Astonishing himself and his seamstresses, Shin lost his composure. He grabbed a large wrench and swung it as hard as he could, trying to crack open Gong's skull. The wrench crunched into his forearm, which Gong raised just in time to protect his head.

Gong yowled and fell to the floor. The shift foreman who had trained Shin rushed over. He found Shin, wild-eyed and wrench in hand, standing over Gong, whose bloody arm had a lump on it the size of an egg. The foreman slapped Shin's face and took his wrench. The seamstresses returned to sewing. From then on, Gong kept his distance.

The garment factory is a sprawling cluster of seven large buildings, all of which are visible on satellite photographs. Located near the Taedong River, its grounds lie at the entrance to Valley 2, not far from the hydroelectric dam and factories that make glassware and porcelain.

During Shin's time at the garment factory, there were dormitories on the grounds for two thousand seamstresses, as well as for five hundred men who worked in sewing machine repair, garment design, plant maintenance, and shipping. The factory superintendent was the only Bowiwon on the site. All the other foremen, including the *chongban-jang,* or head foreman, were prisoners.

Working in the factory put Shin in close daily contact with several hundred women in their teens, twenties, and thirties. Some were strikingly attractive, and their sexuality created tension on the factory floor. Part of it was their ill-fitting uniforms. They had no bras and few wore underwear. Sanitary napkins were not available.

As a twenty-year-old virgin, Shin was nervous around these women. They interested him, but he worried about the camp rule that prescribed death for prisoners who had sexual relations without prior approval. Shin said he was careful not to get involved with any of the women. But the prohibition on sex meant nothing to the factory superintendent and the handful of favored prisoners who served as foremen.

The superintendent, a guard in his thirties, wandered among the seamstresses like a buyer at a cattle auction. Shin watched him choose a different girl every few days, ordering her to clean his room, which was located inside the factory. Seamstresses not cleaning the superintendent's room were fair game for the chief foreman and other prisoners with supervisory jobs in the factory.

Women had no choice but to comply. There was also something in it for them, at least in the short term. If they pleased the superintendent or one of the foremen, they could expect less work and more food. If they broke a sewing machine, they were not beaten.

One seamstress who regularly cleaned the superintendent's room was Park Choon Young, whom Shin knew from secondary school and who operated a sewing machine that he maintained. She was twenty-two and exceptionally pretty. Four months after she began spending afternoons in the superintendent's room, Shin heard from another former school friend that she was pregnant.

Her condition was kept secret until her belly began to poke through her uniform. Then she disappeared.

Shin learned how to tell from a sewing machine's sound what was wrong with it. He was less adept in lugging the bulky machines to the repair shop. In the summer of 2004, while carrying one up a flight of stairs on his back, it slipped from his grasp. The sewing machine tumbled down the stairwell, broken beyond repair.

His immediate superior, the foreman who had been patient with Shin as he learned the ropes in the factory, slapped Shin a few times when he saw the ruined machine. He then reported the damage up the factory's chain of command. Sewing machines were considered more valuable than prisoners, and ruining one was regarded as a grave offense.

A few minutes after he dropped the sewing machine, Shin was called into the office of the plant superintendent, along with the chief foreman and the floor foreman who had reported the incident.

"What were you thinking?" the superintendent shouted at Shin. "Do you want to die? How could you be so weak that you lost your grip? You're always stuffing your face with food."

"Even if you die, the sewing machine can't be brought back," the superintendent added. "Your hand is the problem. Cut his finger off!"

The chief foreman grabbed Shin's right hand and held it down on a table in the superintendent's office. With a kitchen knife, he hacked Shin's middle finger off just above the first knuckle.

Shin's foreman helped him leave the superintendent's office and escorted him back to the factory floor. Later that night, the foreman took Shin to the camp's health center, where a prisoner who worked as a nurse soaked his finger in salt water, stitched it up, and wrapped it in cloth.

That did not keep it from getting infected. But from his time in the underground cell, Shin remembered how Uncle had rubbed salted cabbage soup into his wounds. At mealtimes, Shin soaked his finger in soup. The infection did not spread into the bone and within three months, new skin healed over the stumpy finger.

For the first two days after the injury, Shin's foreman filled in on the factory floor. It was an unexpected gesture of concern that allowed Shin to recover. The kind foreman did not last long on the job. He disappeared, along with his wife, a few months after Shin dropped the sewing machine. Shin heard from other repairmen that the foreman's wife, while out working in the woods, had stumbled upon a secret execution in a mountain gorge.

Before the foreman disappeared, he brought Shin a gift.

"It's rice flour, and your father wants you to have it," the foreman said.

At the mention of his father's name, Shin became angry. Although he had tried to repress it, the resentment he felt toward his mother and brother had grown since their deaths. It had poisoned his feelings for his father. Shin wanted nothing to do with him.

"You eat it," Shin said.

"Your father intended it for you," the foreman replied, looking puzzled. "Shouldn't you eat it?"

Despite his hunger, Shin refused.

With so many prisoners working so close together, the factory was a petri dish for snitching.

A coworker betrayed Shin a few weeks after he dropped the sewing machine. His shift had failed to meet the day's production quota and was required to do bitter humiliation work. Along with three other repairmen, Shin did not get back to his dormitory room until after midnight.

They were all wildly hungry and one suggested they raid the factory's vegetable garden, where there were cabbage, lettuce, cucumbers, eggplant, and radishes. It was raining and there was no moonlight. They figured the chances of being caught were low. They snuck outside, filled their arms with vegetables, and brought them back to their room, where they ate and fell asleep.

In the morning, the four were called to the superintendent's office. Someone had reported their midnight meal. The superintendent whacked each of them on the head with a stick. He then told one repairman, Kang Man Bok, to leave the room. A snitch can smell a snitch; Shin instinctively knew Kang had informed.

The superintendent ordered that rations for the three remaining men be cut in half for two weeks, and he clubbed them on the head a few more times. Returning to the factory, Shin noticed that Kang would not meet his eye.

Soon, Shin was asked to spy on his fellow workers. The superintendent called him to his office and said that to wash away the sins of his mother and brother, he had to report wrongdoers. It took Shin two months before he found one.

Lying sleepless on the floor one night, he watched as a roommate, a transport worker named Kang Chul Min, who was in his late twenties, got up and began mending his work trousers. He used a swatch of military uniform cloth to cover a hole in his pants. He apparently had stolen the cloth from the factory floor.

The following morning, Shin went to the superintendent.

"Teacher, I saw a stolen piece of cloth."

"Really? Who had it?

"It was Kang Chul Min, in my room."

Shin worked late that night in the factory and was among the last of the sewing machine repairmen to walk into a ten o'clock meeting of ideological struggle, a mandatory session of self-criticism.

As he entered the room, he saw Kang Chul Min. He was on his knees and bound in chains. His bare back was covered with welts from a whip. His secret girlfriend, a seamstress whom Shin had heard rumors about, knelt beside him. She, too, was in chains. They remained kneeling in silence throughout the ninety-minute meeting. When it ended, the superintendent ordered each worker to slap Kang and his girlfriend in the face before leaving the room. Shin slapped them both.

He heard that they were then dragged outside and forced to kneel on a concrete floor for several more hours. The two never figured out who had reported the stolen cloth. Shin did his best to avoid their eyes.

CHAPTER 13

DECIDING NOT
TO SNITCH

The superintendent had another job for Shin.

Park Yong Chul, short and stout, with a shock of white hair, was an important new prisoner. He had lived abroad. His wife was well connected. He knew senior people in the North Korean government.

The superintendent ordered Shin to teach Park how to fix sewing machines and to become his friend. Shin was to report back on everything Park said about his past, his politics, and his family.

"Park needs to confess," the superintendent said. "He's holding out on us."

In October 2004, Shin and Park began spending fourteen hours a day together in the garment factory. Park paid polite attention to Shin's instructions on sewing machine maintenance. Just as politely, he avoided questions about his past. Shin learned little.

Then, after four weeks of near silence, Park surprised Shin with a personal question.

"Sir, where is your home?"

"My home?" Shin said. "My home is here."

"I am from Pyongyang, sir," Park said.

Park addressed Shin using honorific nouns and verb endings. In the Korean language, they signified the seniority and superiority of Shin the teacher over Park the apprentice. Park was a dignified man in his mid-forties, but the linguistic fussiness annoyed and embarrassed Shin.

"I'm younger than you," Shin said. "Please drop the honorific with me."

"I will," said Park.

"By the way," asked Shin, "where is Pyongyang?"

Shin's question stunned Park.

The older man, though, did not laugh or make light of Shin's ignorance. He seemed intrigued by it. He carefully explained that Pyongyang, located about fifty miles south of Camp 14, was the capital of North Korea, the city where all the country's powerful people lived.

The ice had been broken by Shin's naïveté. Park began to talk about himself. He said he had grown up in a large, comfortable apartment in Pyongyang and had followed the privileged educational trajectory of North Korea's elites, studying in East Germany and the Soviet Union. After returning home, he had become chief of a taekwondo training center in Pyongyang. In that high-profile job, Park said, he had met many of the men who ruled North Korea.

Touching his oil-stained right hand to a sewing machine, Park said, "With this hand, I shook Kim Jong Il's hand."

Park looked like an athlete. His hands were large and meaty. He was impressively strong, if a bit thick around the middle. But what impressed Shin was Park's decency. He did not make Shin feel stupid. He patiently attempted to explain what life was like outside Camp 14—and outside North Korea.

So began a monthlong one-on-one seminar that would forever change Shin's life.

As they walked the factory floor, Park told Shin that the giant country next door was called China. Its people were rapidly getting rich. He said that in the south there was another Korea. In South Korea, he said, everyone was already rich. Park explained the concept of money. He told Shin about the existence of television and computers and mobile phones. He explained that the world was round.

Much of what Park talked about, especially at the beginning, was difficult for Shin to understand, believe, or care about. Shin wasn't especially interested in how the world worked. What delighted him— what he kept begging Park for—were stories about food and eating, particularly when the main course was grilled meat.

These were the stories that kept Shin up at night fantasizing about a better life. Partly it was the grinding exhaustion of work in the factory. Meals were skimpy, hours were endless, and Shin was always hungry. But there was something more—something buried in Shin's memory from when he was thirteen and struggling to recover from his burns in the underground prison: his aging cellmate had inflamed his imagination with tales of hearty meals. Uncle had dared Shin to dream about one day getting out of the camp and eating whatever he wanted. Freedom, in Shin's mind, was just another word for grilled meat.

While the old man in the underground prison had eaten well in North Korea, Park's gustatory adventures were global. He described the enchantments of chicken, pork, and beef in China, Hong Kong, Germany, England, and the former Soviet Union. The more Shin listened to these stories, the more he wanted out of the camp. He ached for a world where an insignificant person like himself could walk into a restaurant and fill his stomach with rice and meat. He fantasized about escaping with Park because he wanted to eat like Park.

Intoxicated by what he heard from the prisoner he was supposed to betray, Shin made perhaps the first free decision of his life. He chose not to snitch.

It marked a major shift in his calculations about how to survive. Based on Shin's experience, snitching paid. It saved him from the executioners who had killed his mother and brother. After the execution, it may have been the reason his secondary school teacher made sure he had food, put a stop to the hazing, and assigned him to an easy job on the pig farm.

But Shin's decision to honor Park's confidences did not signify new insight into the nature of right and wrong. Looking back, Shin views his behavior as fundamentally selfish. If he informed on Park, he could have earned an extra serving of cabbage. Perhaps he might have been promoted to foreman, with a special dispensation to prey upon the seamstresses.

But Park's stories were much more valuable to Shin. They had become an essential and energizing addiction, changing his expectations about the future and giving him the will to plan for it. He believed he would go mad without hearing more.

In his reports to the superintendent, Shin found himself telling a wonderfully liberating lie. Park, he said, had nothing to say.

A decade earlier in the underground prison, Shin's aging cellmate had dared to talk about food outside the camp. But Uncle had never talked about himself or his politics. He was careful, suspicious, and withholding. He guessed Shin was an informer and did not trust him. Shin took no offense. He saw it as normal. Trust was a good way to get shot.

But after Park's initial reticence, he was not suspicious. In the apparent belief that Shin was as trustworthy as he was ignorant, Park told his life story.

Park said he lost his position as head of taekwondo training in Pyongyang in 2002, after squabbling with a midlevel apparatchik who apparently snitched on him to higher-ups in the government. Without a job, Park traveled north to the border with his wife, where they ille-gally crossed into China and stayed with his uncle for eighteen months. They intended to return to Pyongyang, where they had left behind a teenage child who lived with Park's parents.

While in China, Park listened daily to radio broadcasts from South Korea. He paid close attention to coverage of Hwang Jang Yop, a prin-cipal architect of North Korea's ideology and the highest-ranking offi-cial ever to defect. Hwang, who fled in 1997, had become a celebrity in Seoul.

As Shin and Park did their rounds in the garment factory, Park explained that Hwang had criticized Kim Jong Il for turning North Korea into a corrupt feudal state. (Kim's government dispatched agents in 2010 to try to assassinate Hwang. The agents, however, were arrested in Seoul, and Hwang died of natural causes that year, at eighty-seven.)

Park left China and returned to North Korea in the summer of 2003, along with his wife and a baby son born in China. He wanted to get back to Pyongyang in time to vote in the August election for the Supreme People's Assembly, the rubber stamp parliament of North Korea.

Elections in North Korea are empty rituals. Candidates are chosen by the Korean Workers' Party and run without opposition. But Park feared that if he missed the vote, the government would notice his absence, declare him to be a traitor, and send his family to a labor camp. Voting in North Korea is not mandatory, but the government keeps close track of those who do not show up.

At the border, North Korean authorities detained Park and his family. He tried to convince them that he wasn't a defector, that he had merely been visiting family in China and was coming home to vote. Authorities did not buy it. They accused him of being a convert to Christianity and a spy for South Korea. After several rounds of interrogation, Park and his wife and son were sent to Camp 14. Park was assigned to the camp's textile factory in the autumn of 2004.

When Shin met him, Park was furious with himself for returning to North Korea. His foolishness had cost him his freedom, and, as he told Shin, it would soon cost him his wife.

She was divorcing him. She came from a prominent family in Pyongyang with strong party connections, Park said, and she was trying to convince camp guards that she had been a loyal and submissive wife, while her husband was a political criminal.

Despite Park's anger—at the rottenness of North Korea, at his wife, at himself—he always carried himself with dignity, especially when it was time to eat.

Shin found this utterly amazing. Everyone he knew in the camp behaved like a panicked animal at mealtimes. Park, even when hungry, did not. When Shin caught rats in the factory, Park insisted on patience. He refused to allow Shin to eat them until they'd found a furnace or flame where a rat could be spread out on the head of a shovel and cooked properly.

Park could also be a blithe spirit. In Shin's view, he sometimes took this a bit too far.

Take, for example, Park's singing.

In the middle of a night shift on the floor of the factory, Park alarmed Shin by bursting into song.

"Hey! What do you think you are doing?" Shin asked, fearing that a foreman might hear.

"Singing," Park said.

"Stop at once," Shin told him.

Shin had never sung a song. His only exposure to music had been on the farm, when trucks with loudspeakers played martial music while prisoners picked weeds. To Shin, singing seemed unnatural and insanely risky.

"Would you like to sing with me?" Park asked.

Shin vigorously shook his head and waved his hands, trying to silence Park.

"Who would hear me at this hour?" Park said. "Sing after me this once."

Shin refused.

Park asked why he was so afraid of a little song when he was willing to hear seditious stories about how Kim Jong Il was a thief and North Korea was a hellhole.

Shin explained that he tolerated such things because Park had the good sense to whisper. "I wish you wouldn't sing," Shin said.

Park agreed not to. But a few nights later, he again broke into song and offered to teach Shin the lyrics. Although dubious and afraid, Shin listened and sang with Park, but quietly.

The lyrics of "Song of the Winter Solstice," which recent defectors say is the theme song of a popular program on North Korean state television, are about traveling companions who endure hardship and pain.

As we all walk down life's long, long road,

We will remain warm traveling companions, standing against the lashes of wind and rain.

Along that road there will be happiness and suffering.

We will overcome; we will endure all of life's tempests.

It is still the only song Shin knows.

———

In November, not long after Park was assigned to the textile factory, four Bowiwon guards paid a surprise visit to the prisoners' nightly meeting of self-criticism. Two of them were unfamiliar faces, and Shin believed they were from outside the camp.

As the meeting ended, the chief guard said he wanted to talk about lice, a chronic problem in the camps. He asked prisoners to step forward if they were infested.

A man and a woman who were leaders in their respective dormitory rooms stood. They said lice were out of control in their quarters. Guards gave each of them a bucket filled with a cloudy liquid that smelled, to Shin, like agricultural chemicals.

To demonstrate its effectiveness in controlling lice, guards asked five men and five women in each of the infested dorm rooms to wash themselves with the cloudy liquid. Shin and Park, of course, had lice, but they were not given an opportunity to use the treatment.

In about a week, all ten prisoners who had been washing with the liquid developed boils on their skin. After several weeks, their skin began to putrefy and flake off. They had high fevers that kept them from working. Shin saw a truck arrive at the factory and watched as the ailing prisoners were loaded into it. He never saw them again.

It was then, in mid-December 2004, that Shin decided he had had enough. He began thinking about escape.

Park made those thoughts possible. He changed the way Shin connected with other people. Their friendship broke a lifelong pattern— stretching back to Shin's malignant relationship with his mother—of wariness and betrayal.

Shin was no longer a creature of his captors. He believed he had found someone to help him survive.

Their relationship echoed, in many ways, the bonds of trust and mutual protection that kept prisoners alive and sane in Nazi concentration camps. In those camps, researchers found, the "basic unit of survival" was the pair, not the individual.

"[I]t was in the pairs that the prisoners kept alive the semblance of humanity," concluded Elmer Luchterhand, a sociologist at Yale who interviewed fifty-two concentration camp survivors shortly after liberation.[1]

Pairs stole food and clothing for each other, exchanged small gifts, and planned for the future. If one member of a pair fainted from hunger in front of an SS officer, the other would prop him up.

"Survival . . . could only be a social achievement, not an individual accident," wrote Eugene Weinstock, a Belgian resistance fighter and Hungarian-born Jew who was sent to Buchenwald in 1943.[2]

The death of one member of a pair often doomed the other. Women who knew Anne Frank in the Bergen-Belsen camp said that neither hunger nor typhus killed the young girl who would become the most famous diarist of the Nazi era. Rather, they said, she lost the will to live after the death of her sister, Margot.[3]

Like Nazi concentration camps, labor camps in North Korea use confinement, hunger, and fear to create a kind of Skinner box, a closed, closely regulated chamber in which guards assert absolute control over prisoners.[4] Yet while Auschwitz existed for only three years, Camp 14 is a fifty-year-old Skinner box, an ongoing longitudinal experiment in repression and mind control in which guards breed prisoners whom they control, isolate, and pit against one another from birth.

The miracle of Shin's friendship with Park is how quickly it blew up the box.

Park's spirit, his dignity, and his incendiary information gave Shin something that was both enthralling and unbearable: a context, a way to dream about the future.

He suddenly understood where he was and what he was missing.

Camp 14 was no longer home. It was an abhorrent cage.

And Shin now had a well-traveled, broad-shouldered friend to help him get out.

CHAPTER 14

PREPARING TO RUN

Their plan was simple—and insanely optimistic.

Shin knew the camp. Park knew the world. Shin would get them over the fence. Park would lead them to China, where his uncle would give them shelter, money, and assistance in traveling on to South Korea.

Shin was the first to suggest that they escape together. But before he broached the idea, he fretted for days, fearing that Park might be an informer, that he was being set up, that he would be executed like his mother and brother. Even after Park embraced the idea, Shin's paranoia was difficult to shake: he had sold out his own mother; why shouldn't Park sell him out?

Still, the escape plan, such as it was, went forward as Shin's excitement overcame his fear. He would wake up in high spirits after a night of dreaming about grilled meat. Carrying sewing machines up and down factory stairs no longer wore him out. For the first time in his life, Shin had something to look forward to.

Since Park was under orders to follow Shin around, every working day became a marathon session of whispered escape preparations and motivational stories about the fine dining that awaited them in China.

They decided that if guards discovered them at the fence, Park would take them out using taekwondo. Although guards carry automatic weapons, Shin and Park persuaded each other that their chances of not getting killed were good.

By any measure, these expectations were absurd. No one had escaped from Camp 14. Indeed, just two people other than Shin are known to have escaped from any political prison camp in North Korea and made it to the West. One is Kim Yong, the former lieutenant colonel who had highly placed friends across North Korea. But he did not go over the fence. He escaped because of what he described as a "totally miraculous chance." In 1999, during the governmental breakdown and security lapses that marked the height of the North Korean famine, he hid under a metal panel wedged into the bottom of a dilapidated train car that was being loaded with coal. When the train rolled out of Camp 18, so did Kim, who knew the countryside well and used his personal contacts at the border to find a safe way to cross into China.

The other escapee is Kim Hye Sook, who also fled Camp 18. Along with her family, she was first imprisoned in that camp in 1975, at the age of thirteen. Authorities released her in 2001, but later sent her back to Camp 18. She then escaped, and in 2009 found her way out of North Korea to South Korea, via China, Laos, and Thailand.

Kim Yong had fled a prison that was not nearly as well guarded as the one where Shin and Park were planning their escape. As he wrote in his memoir, *Long Road Home*, he could never have escaped from Camp 14 because "the guards there acted as if they were on a war front."[1] Before Kim was transferred to the camp he eventually escaped from, he says he spent two years in Camp 14. He described the conditions there as "so severe that I could not even think of the possibility" of flight.

Shin and Park were unaware of Kim Yong's escape, and they had no way to gauge the odds of getting out of Camp 14 or of finding safe passage to China. But Park was inclined to believe the radio broadcasts from Seoul, which he had heard while living in China. Those reports focused on the failures and weaknesses of the North Korea government. Park told Shin that the United Nations had begun to criticize human rights violations inside the North's political labor camps. He also said he had heard that the camps would disappear in the not too distant future.[2]

Although Park was well traveled in North Korea and in China, he confided to Shin that he knew little about the steep, snowy, thinly populated mountains outside the fence. Nor did he know much about roads that could lead them safely to China.

Shin knew the layout of the camp from countless days of gathering wood and collecting acorns, but he knew nothing about how to get over or through the high-voltage fence surrounding the camp. Shin did not know if touching wires in the fence would kill them, although he worried about it.

He also found it difficult, during the weeks and days before the escape, to avoid thoughts of what had happened to his mother and brother. It wasn't guilt he felt. It was fear. He feared he would die as they had died. His mind flashed to images of their executions. He imagined standing in front of a firing squad or on a wooden box with a noose around his neck.

Making a calculation that was short on information and long on aspiration, Shin told himself he had a ninety percent chance of getting through the fence and a ten percent chance of getting shot.

Shin's primary preescape preparation was to steal warm clothes, along with new shoes, from a fellow prisoner.

That prisoner slept on the same dormitory floor and worked in the factory as a garment cutter, a job that allowed him to accumulate scraps of fabric, which he traded for food and other goods. He was also meticulous about his clothes. Unlike anyone in the camp, the cutter had assembled a complete extra set of winter clothing and shoes.

Shin had never stolen clothing from another prisoner. But since he stopped snitching, he had become increasingly intolerant of prisoners who continued to inform on their neighbors. He particularly disliked the cutter, who reported on everyone who stole food from the factory garden. Shin thought he deserved to be robbed.

Since prisoners did not have access to lockers or any other way of securing their belongings, it was a simple matter for Shin to wait for the cutter to leave the dormitory room, take his clothes and shoes, and hide them until the escape. The cutter did not suspect Shin when the clothes went missing. The stolen shoes did not fit Shin's feet (shoes in the camp almost never did), but they were relatively new.

Clothing in the camp was distributed only every six months. By late December, when Shin and Park were planning their escape, Shin's winter-season pants had holes in the knees and in the seat. When it came time to run, he decided that for warmth he would wear his old clothes beneath his stolen clothes. He did not have a coat, hat, or gloves to protect him from the bitter cold.

Planning to escape meant waiting for a work detail that would get Shin and Park out of the factory and give them an excuse to be near the fence.

Their chance came on New Year's Day, a rare holiday when machines in the factory went silent for two days. Shin learned in late December that on January 2, the second day of the closure, his crew of sewing machine repairmen and some of the seamstresses would leave the factory and be escorted to a mountain ridge on the eastern edge of

SHIN DONG-HYUK moved in 2009 from South Korea to Southern California, where he worked with Liberty in North Korea (LiNK), a human rights group. He later lived in Seattle, where this photo was taken in 2011.

KIM JONG EUN, leader of North Korea, is Shin's age. The little-known third and youngest son of Kim Jong Il first appeared before the world's press in 2010. After his father's death a year later, North Korean state media hailed him as "another leader sent from heaven."

KYODO VIA AP IMAGES

After seventeen years in power, **KIM JONG IL** died of a heart attack in 2011. The Dear Leader, who inherited his dictatorship from his father, suffered a stroke in 2008. He then began grooming his son Kim Jong Eun to take control.

KIM IL SUNG was North Korea's founding dictator and remains its Eternal President, despite his death in 1994. In this undated official photograph, he gives his famous "on the spot" guidance in the Grand People's Study House, the country's central library.

This hagiographic depiction of **KIM JONG IL** is one of countless paintings, photographs, and statues of the "Dear Leader" that are prominently displayed—and carefully maintained—across North Korea.

The cult of personality surrounding the Kim family began with the Great Leader, **KIM IL SUNG**, who was depicted in government propaganda as a loving father to his people. Although his leadership was brutal, his death in 1994 was deeply mourned.

The teachers at Shin's school in Camp 14 were uniformed guards who always carried pistols. Shin saw one of them beat a six-year-old classmate to death with a chalkboard pointer.

Children in the camps scavenged constantly for food, eating rats, insects, and undigested kernels of corn they found in cow dung.

Shin watched as his mother was hanged and his brother shot for planning to escape.

After the discovery of his mother and brother's escape plan, Shin was held for seven months in a secret underground prison inside Camp 14. He was thirteen years old.

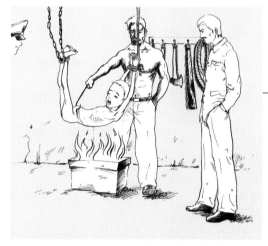

In the underground prison, guards tortured Shin over a coal fire, seeking to find out his role in the planned escape of his mother and brother.

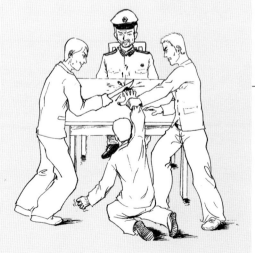

As punishment for dropping a sewing machine while working at a garment factory in the camp, guards used a knife to cut off Shin's right middle finger at the first knuckle.

SHIN returns often to South Korea, where he tries to raise awareness about the North's labor camps. In this 2009 photo, Shin walks in front of a temple in central Seoul.

LOUIS VUITTON

The author conducted interviews with Shin in South Korea, Southern California, and Seattle, Washington. In this 2009 photo, **SHIN** and **HARDEN** stand in front of a Louis Vuitton shop in Seoul.

In Torrance, California, **SHIN** shared a residence with interns working at LiNK, the human rights group. He liked the semichaotic camaraderie of group houses, where up to sixteen young people lived and ate together.

LOWELL AND LINDA DYE of Columbus, Ohio, paid for Shin's move from South Korea to California after reading a *Washington Post* story about his life. Shin calls them "Dad and Mom." This 2009 photo was taken in New York City at a human rights event.

SHIN'S adjustment to life outside Camp 14 has been halting. "I am evolving from being an animal," he says. "But it is going very, very slowly. Sometimes I try to cry and laugh like other people, just to see if it feels like anything." This 2008 photo was taken in Seoul.

the camp. There, they would spend the day trimming trees and stacking wood.

Shin had worked on that mountain before. It was near the fence that ran along the top of the ridge. Apprised of all this, Park agreed they would escape on January 2, 2005.

When the factory shut down on January 1, Shin decided, with some reluctance, to pay a final visit to his father.

Their relationship, always distant, had grown colder still. Shin, on the few days when he did not have to work on the farm or in the factory, had rarely taken advantage of camp rules that allowed him to visit. Spending time with his father had become an ordeal.

What made Shin so angry with his father was not clear, at least not to Shin. It was his mother, not his father, who had put his life at risk by plotting an escape when he was thirteen. She and Shin's brother were the ones who had been complicit in starting a chain of events that resulted in his arrest, torture, and hazing in secondary school. His father had been another victim.

But his father was alive and attempting a reconciliation with Shin. By the unforgiving calculus of relations between distant fathers and resentful sons, that was reason enough for Shin's loathing.

They shared a sullen New Year's supper in a cafeteria at his father's work site, eating cornmeal and cabbage soup. Shin made no reference to his escape plan. He had told himself, as he walked to see his father, that any show of emotions, any hint of final leave-taking could imperil the escape. He did not completely trust him.

His father had tried, after the killing of his wife and eldest son, to be more attentive. He had apologized for being a bad parent and for having exposed the boy to the camp's savagery. He had even encouraged his son, if he ever got the chance, to "see what the world is like." That lukewarm escape endorsement may have been blandly worded because Shin's father did not completely trust his son, either.

After Shin was assigned to the garment factory, where opportunities to find or steal extra food were particularly meager, his father had gone to the extraordinary trouble of obtaining the rice flour and sending it to his son as a paternal offering. Shin was repulsed by his father's gift and, although hungry, gave it away.

When they sat together in the cafeteria now, neither mentioned that gift, and when Shin left that evening, there was no special goodbye. He expected that when guards learned of the escape, they would come for his father and take him back to the underground prison. He was nearly certain that his father did not know what was coming.

CHAPTER 15

THE FENCE

Early the next morning, a foreman from the garment factory herded Shin, Park, and about twenty-five other prisoners up the mountain. They set to work near the top of a twelve-hundred-foot slope. The sky was clear and the sun shone brightly on a heavy snow pack, but it was cold and the wind was blowing. Some prisoners used small axes to hack the branches off logged trees, while others stacked wood.

The firewood detail was an extraordinary stroke of good luck. It placed Shin and Park within a stone's throw of the fence that ran along the spine of the mountain. On the far side of that fence, the terrain cants steeply down, but it is not too steep to be traversed by foot. Not far beyond the fence there is tree cover.

A guard tower rose from the fence line about a quarter mile to the north of where the prisoners chopped wood. Guards, walking two abreast, patrolled the inside perimeter of the fence. Shin noticed lengthy intervals between patrols.

The foreman in charge of the work crew was also a prisoner, and therefore unarmed. In the intervals between guard patrols, there was no one close who could fire a weapon at Shin and Park. They had decided earlier that they would bide their time until dusk, when it would be more difficult for guards to track their footsteps in the snow.

As Shin worked and waited, he brooded about how the other prisoners were oblivious to the fence and the opportunities that lay beyond it. They were like cows, he thought, with a cud-chewing passivity, resigned to their no-exit lives. He had been like them until he met Park.

At around four o'clock, with light draining out of the day, Shin and Park sidled toward the fence, trimming trees as they moved. No one seemed to notice.

Shin soon found himself facing the fence, which was about ten feet high. There was a knee-high berm of snow directly in front of him and then a trail where patrolling guards had tramped it down. Beyond that was a groomed strip of sand. It showed footprints if someone stepped on it. And beyond that was the fence itself, which consisted of seven or eight strands of high-voltage barbed wire, spaced about a foot apart, strung between tall poles.

The fences that surround some of the labor camps in North Korea include moats with spikes designed to impale anyone who falls in, according to Kwon Hyuk, a defector who worked as a manager at Camp 22. But Shin saw no moat and no spikes.

He and Park had told each other that if they could get through the fence without touching the wires, they would be fine. As to how they might be able to do that, they were not sure. Yet as the hour of the escape drew nearer, Shin surprised himself by not feeling afraid.

Park, though, was distracted.

After guards had passed along the fence as part of their late-afternoon patrol, Shin heard fear in Park's voice.

"I don't know if I can do this," he whispered. "Can't we try it some other time?"

"What are you talking about," Shin said. "If we don't do it now, there won't be another chance."

Shin feared it would be months, even years before they would be allowed outside the factory at dusk near a section of fence that could not be seen from a guard tower.

He could not—would not—endure more waiting.

"Let's run!" he yelled.

He grabbed Park's hand and pulled him toward the fence. For an agonizing second or two, Shin had to drag the man who had inspired his desire to escape. Soon, though, Park began to run.

Their plan had been for Shin to stay in the lead until they got clear of the fence, but he slipped and fell to his knees on the icy patrol trail.

Park was first to the fence. Falling to his knees, he shoved his arms, head, and shoulders between the two lowest strands of wire.

Seconds later, Shin saw sparks and smelled burning flesh.

Most electric fences built for security purposes repel trespassers with a painful but exceedingly brief pulse of current. They are not designed to kill, but to frighten animals and people. Lethal electric fences, however, use a continuous current that can make a person lock on to the wire as voltage causes involuntary muscle contractions, paralysis, and death.

Before Shin could get to his feet, Park had stopped moving. He may already have been dead. The weight of his body pulled down the bottom strand of wire, pinning it against the snowy ground and creating a small gap in the fence.

Without hesitation, Shin crawled over his friend's body, using it as a kind of insulating pad. As he squirmed through the fence, Shin could feel the current. The soles of his feet felt as though needles were stabbing them.

Shin was nearly through the fence when his lower legs slipped off

Park's torso and came into direct contact, through the two pairs of pants he was wearing, with the bottom strand. Voltage from the wire caused severe burns from his ankles to his knees. The wounds bled for weeks.

But it would be a couple hours before Shin noticed how badly he had been injured.

What he remembers most clearly about crawling through the fence was that Park's body smelled like it was burning.

The human body is unpredictable when it comes to conducting electricity. For reasons that are not well understood, the ability of individuals to sustain and survive a high-voltage shock varies widely. It is not a matter of build or fitness. Stout people show no greater resistance than skinny ones.

Human skin can be a relatively good insulator, if it is dry. Cold weather closes skin pores, reducing conductivity. Multiple layers of clothing can also help. Yet sweaty hands and wet clothes can easily defeat the skin's natural resistance to current. Once high-voltage electricity penetrates a body that is well grounded (wet shoes on snowy ground), the liquids and salts in blood, muscle, and bone are excellent conductors. Wet people holding hands have died of electrocution together.

Shin's success in crawling through an electric fence designed to kill seems to have been a function of luck. His was astoundingly good; Park's was terrible. If Shin had not slipped in the snow, he would have reached the fence first and he probably would have died.

Shin did not know it, but to pass safely through the fence he needed a device that could shunt the flow of current from the fence to the ground. Park's body, lying on damp ground atop the bottom strand of wire, became that device.

With Park siphoning off current and funneling it to the ground, the level of voltage that Shin was exposed to as he crawled over his friend's back was probably not close to being lethal. The extra layers of clothing he wore may also have helped.

When he cleared the fence, he had no idea where to go. At the crest of the mountain, the only direction he could comprehend was down. At first, he weaved through a patch of trees. But within minutes, he was out in the open, stumbling across upland fields and pastures that were sporadically lit by a half moon showing through clouds.

He ran for about two hours, always heading downhill, until he entered a mountain valley. There were barns and scattered houses. He heard no alarms, no gunfire, no shouting. As far as he could tell, no one was chasing him.

As the adrenaline of flight began to ebb, Shin noticed that the legs of his pants were sticky. He rolled them up, saw blood oozing out of his legs, and began to comprehend the severity of his burns. His feet, too, were bleeding. He had stepped on nails, apparently when he was close to the camp fence. It was very cold, well below 10 degrees Fahrenheit. He had no coat.

Park, dead on the fence, had not told him where he might find China.

CHAPTER 16

STEALING

Racing downhill in early evening darkness through cornfield stubble, Shin came across a farmer's shed half buried in the hillside. The door was locked. There were no houses nearby, so he broke the lock with an ax handle he found on the ground.

Just inside the door, he discovered three ears of dried corn and devoured them. The corn made him aware of how hungry he was. Helped by moonlight, he searched the shed for something else to eat. Instead, he spotted an old pair of cotton shoes and a worn military uniform.

Uniforms are everywhere in North Korea, the world's most militarized society. Conscription is almost universal. Men serve ten years, women seven. With more than a million troops on active duty, about five percent of the country's population is in uniform, compared with about half of one percent in the United States. An additional five million people serve in the army reserve for much of their adult lives. The army is "the people, the state, and the party," says the government, which no longer describes itself as a communist state. Its guiding principle, according to the constitution, is "military first." Uniformed soldiers dig clams and launch missiles, pick apples and build irrigation canals, market mushrooms and supervise the export of knockoff Nintendo games.

Inevitably, uniforms wind up in barns and sheds.

The military pants and shirt that Shin found were far too big for him, as were the cotton shoes. But finding a change of clothes—less than three hours after escaping the camp and before anyone could get a look at him—was an extraordinary stroke of luck.

He stepped out of his cold wet shoes and removed both pairs of prison trousers. From the knees down they were stiff with blood and snow. He tried to bandage the burns on his legs with ripped-out pages from a book he found in the shed. The pages stuck to his mangled shins. He put on the ratty, too-big uniform and slipped his feet into the cotton shoes.

No longer instantly recognizable as a runaway prisoner, he had become just another ill-clothed, ill-shod, and ill-nourished North Korean. In a country where a third of the population were chronically malnourished, where local markets and train stations were crowded with filthy itinerant traders, and where almost everyone has served in the army, Shin easily blended in.

Outside the shed, he also found a road, and he followed it down into a village at the bottom of the valley. There, to his surprise, he saw the Taedong River.

For all his running, he was only two miles upstream from Camp 14.

News of his escape had not reached the village. Streets were dark and empty. Shin crossed a bridge over the Taedong and headed east on a road parallel to the river. He hid from headlights when a single car drove by. Then he climbed up to a railroad track that seemed deserted and kept walking.

By late evening, he had walked about six miles and entered the outskirts of Bukchang, a coal town just south of the river with a population of about ten thousand people. A few pedestrians were out, but Shin did not sense that his presence warranted special attention. With an aluminum factory, coal mines, and a large power plant, the town was perhaps accustomed to night-shift workers walking the streets at all hours.

Shin saw a pigpen, a familiar and comforting sight. He crawled over a fence, found some rice straw, and dug in for the night.

For the next two days, Shin scavenged around the outskirts of Bukchang, eating whatever he could find on the ground or in garbage heaps. He had no idea what to do or where to go. People in the street seemed to ignore him. His legs hurt, and he was hungry and cold. Yet he was exhilarated. He felt like an alien fallen to earth.

In the months and years ahead, Shin would discover all things modern: streaming video, blogs, and international air travel. Therapists and career counselors would advise him. Preachers would show him how to pray to Jesus Christ. Friends would teach him how to brush his teeth, use a debit card, and fool around with a smartphone. From obsessive reading online, the politics, history, and geography of the two Koreas, China, Southeast Asia, Europe, and the United States would all become familiar.

None of this, though, did more to change his understanding of how the world works—and how human beings interact with each other— than his first days outside the camp.

It shocked him to see North Koreans going about their daily lives without having to take orders from guards. When they had the temerity to laugh together in the streets or wear brightly colored clothes or haggle over prices in an open-air market, he expected armed men to step in, knock heads, and stop the nonsense.

The word Shin uses again and again to describe those first days is "shock."

It was not meaningful to him that North Korea in the dead of winter is ugly, dirty, and dark, or that it is poorer than Sudan, or that, taken as a whole, it is viewed by human rights groups as the world's largest prison.

His context had been twenty-three years in an open-air cage run by men who hanged his mother, shot his brother, crippled his father, murdered pregnant women, beat children to death, taught him to betray his family, and tortured him over a fire.

He felt wonderfully free—and, as best he could determine, no one was looking for him.

But he was also weak with hunger, and as he wandered the streets, he began searching for an empty house where he could eat and rest. He found one at the end of a small road. Tearing open a rear window made of vinyl, he climbed inside.

In the kitchen, he found three bowls of cooked rice. He guessed someone who would soon return had prepared it. Afraid to risk eating or sleeping in the house, he emptied the rice into a plastic bag and spooned in some soybean paste he found on a shelf.

Searching the rest of the house, he found a pair of winter-weight trousers draped over a hanger and another pair of shoes. He also found a rucksack and a dark brown winter coat, which was military in style and much warmer than any coat he had ever worn. He opened one last kitchen drawer and found a ten-pound bag of rice. He stuffed it in the rucksack and left.

Near the center of Bukchang, a market lady shouted at him. She wanted to know what was in his rucksack, if he had anything to sell. Trying to keep calm, Shin said he had some rice. She offered to buy it for four thousand North Korean won, which was worth about four dollars at black-market exchange rates.

Shin had first learned about the existence of money from Park. Before the market lady yelled at him, he had watched in wonder as people used small pieces of paper—he guessed it was money—to buy food and other goods.

He had no idea if four thousand won was a fair price for his stolen rice, but he happily sold it and bought some crackers and cookies. He pocketed the remaining money and left town on foot. His destination was China, but he still did not know where it might be.

On the road, Shin encountered several worn-looking men and eavesdropped on their conversations. They were searching for work, scrounging for food, traveling among street markets, and trying to steer clear of the police. One or two of them asked Shin where he was from. He said he had grown up in the Bukchang area, which was true enough and seemed to satisfy their curiosity.

Shin soon figured out that most of these men were strangers to one another. But he was afraid to ask too many questions. He did not want to feel an obligation to talk about himself.

The people wandering around inside North Korea at that time were mostly unemployed laborers and failed farmers, according to a survey of more than thirteen hundred North Korean refugees that was conducted in China in late 2004 and 2005.[1] There were also students, soldiers, technicians, and a few former government officials.

The survey suggested they were on the road primarily for economic reasons, hoping to find work or trade in China. Their lives had been exceedingly difficult and their relationship with the government was strained: nearly a quarter of the men and thirty-seven percent of the women said family members had died of hunger. More than a quarter of them had been arrested in North Korea, and ten percent said they had been sent to jails, where forced starvation, torture, and executions were commonplace. To get out of North Korea, more than half of the refugees said they paid cash to bribe officials or buy help from professional smugglers.

Shin fell in with these wanderers, guessing he would be safer in their company than traveling by himself. He tried to pattern his behavior after the men he met on the road. It was not difficult. Like him, they dressed shabbily, looked dirty, smelled bad, and were desperate for food.

As a police state, North Korea does not tolerate intercity vagabonds. Laws strictly prohibit citizens from traveling between cities without proper authorization. But in the aftermath of the famine—with the collapse of the state-run economy, the rise of private markets, and the near ubiquity of traders hustling around the country with goods smuggled from China—laws were often ignored. Police could be bribed; indeed, many lived off bribes. Vagabonds with a bit of cash could travel toward China without attracting attention.

There are no reliable numbers on defections to China, or on the movement of people drifting around inside North Korea. The odds of avoiding arrest and successfully crossing to China seem to change from season to season. It depends on how recently the North Korean government has ordered a security crackdown, how vigilant Chinese authorities are in repatriating defectors, how willing border guards are to take bribes, and how desperate North Koreans are to cross the border. The North Korean government has created new labor camps to hold traders and travelers too poor or too unlucky to bribe their way north.

One trend, though, is clear. The number of North Koreans seeking asylum in South Korea has increased nearly every year since 1995. Forty-one arrived in 1995. By 2009, the number had jumped to nearly three thousand. More defectors turned up in the South between 2005 and 2011 than had fled North Korea over the entire period since the end of the Korean War in 1953.

When Shin began walking toward the border in January 2005, conditions for escape seem to have been relatively good. Numerical evidence can be found in the large number of North Koreans—about forty-five hundred—who arrived in South Korea in 2006 and 2007. It usually takes a year or two for defectors to find their way from China to South Korea.

The permeability of North Korea's border tends to improve when border guards and local officials can accept bribes without draconian punishment from higher-ups.

"More than ever, money talks," said Chun Ki-won, a minister in Seoul who told me that between 2000 and 2008 he had helped more than six hundred North Koreans cross into China and make their way to South Korea.

By the time Shin crawled through the electric fence, there was a well-established human smuggling network with tentacles that reached deep inside North Korea. Chun and several other Seoul-based operatives told me that given enough money they could get virtually any North Korean out of the country.

Using word of mouth, brokers in Seoul offered "planned escapes." A low-budget version cost less than two thousand dollars. It involved months or years of travel through China, via Thailand or Vietnam, to Seoul, and it could require treacherous river crossings, arduous travel on foot, and weeks of waiting in an unsanitary Thai refugee camp.

A first-class planned escape, complete with a forged Chinese passport and an air ticket from Beijing to Seoul, sold for ten thousand dollars or more. From start to finish, brokers and defectors said, going first class could take as little as three weeks.

Activist pastors from South Korean churches invented the escape trade in the late 1990s and early 2000s, hiring border operatives who greased the palms of North Korean guards with cash donated by parishioners in Seoul. By the time Shin hit the road, defectors themselves, many of them former North Korean military and police officers, had taken over the trade and were quietly running for-profit operations.

This new breed of brokers would often receive advance payment in cash from affluent or middle-income South Korean families seeking the release of a relative. They sometimes worked on the installment plan, taking little or no money up front from a defector or his family. When an installment-plan defector arrived in Seoul and had access to some of the more than forty thousand dollars that the South Korean government gives to new arrivals from the North, brokers usually demanded far more money than their basic fee.

"My boss is willing to put up all the money to pay bribes to get someone out," said a Seoul-based broker and former North Korean military officer who worked for a smuggling operation based in China. "But when you get to Seoul, you have to pay double for this service."

By 2008, many North Korean defectors were so deeply in debt to the smugglers that the South Korean government changed the way it distributed cash support. Instead of lump-sum payments, the money was paid out over time, with incentives for those who found and held jobs. About a quarter of the money went directly for housing, eliminating any chance that it could be paid to a broker.

Using their personal and institutional contacts in the North, brokers hired guides to escort people from their homes in North Korea to the Chinese border, where they were handed over to Chinese-speaking guides, who drove them to Beijing Airport.

Outside Seoul, I talked to a North Korean defector who had paid twelve thousand dollars to a broker to smuggle out her eleven-year-old son in 2002.

"I didn't know it could happen so fast," said the mother, who did not want to disclose her name because she and her siblings were paying another broker to smuggle out their mother at the time. "It took only five days for my son to be plucked out and taken across the river into China. I was dumbfounded when I got a call from officials at Seoul airport to tell me my son was here."

At the border and inside the country, the North Korean government has tried to crush these smuggling operations—and periodically it succeeds.

"A lot of people get caught," Lee Jeong Yeon, a former North Korean border officer, told me. "The policy is for one hundred percent execution of those caught helping people to defect. I personally saw several such executions. The successful brokers are experienced people who have good contacts in the military, and they bribe the guards," he said. "Guards are rotated often, and new people have to be bribed."

Lee, whose identity was confirmed by South Korean intelligence officials, worked for three years along the China–North Korea border. He supervised undercover agents who pretended to be brokers and guides in order to infiltrate and disrupt the smuggling trade. After his defection to the South, Lee told me he had used his contacts in the North to smuggle out thirty-four people to freedom.

Shin did not have the awareness, the money, or the contacts to use smuggling networks, and he certainly did not have anyone outside the country to engage professionals on his behalf.

But by keeping his mouth shut and his eyes open he entered the slipstream of smuggling, trading, and petty bribery that had become North Korea's postfamine economy.

Traders showed him haystacks where he could sleep, neighborhoods where he could break into houses, and markets where he could trade stolen goods for food. Shin often shared food with them in the evening as they all huddled around roadside fires.

As he walked out of Bukchang that day, wearing his newly stolen coat and carrying a small cache of cookies, Shin joined a small group of traders that by chance was going north.

CHAPTER 17
RIDING NORTH

Unless he could get far away—and quickly—Shin feared he would soon be caught.

He walked nine miles to a small mountain town called Maengsan, where traders told him that a truck would show up near the central market. For a small fee, it hauled passengers to the train station in Hamhung, the second largest city in North Korea.

Shin had not yet learned enough geography to know where Hamhung was. But he did not care. He was desperate to find a means of transportation other than his aching legs. It had been three days since he had crawled through the electric fence, and he was still only about fifteen miles from Camp 14.

After queuing up with traders waiting for the truck, he managed to pile into the back. The road was bad and the sixty-mile journey to Hamhung took all day and into the night. In the back of the truck, a couple of men asked Shin where he had come from and where he was headed. Unsure who they were or why they were asking, Shin feigned confusion and said nothing. The men lost interest and ignored him.

Unknown to him, Shin's travel timing was excellent.

Intercity travel in North Korea had once been impossible without a travel permit, which would be stamped or folded into a "citizen's cer-tificate," a passport-size document modeled after the old Soviet identi-fication card.

Camp-bred prisoners like Shin were never issued a citizen's cer-tificate. For North Koreans who did not have them, travel permits were hard to come by. Travel permits were usually issued for work-related reasons or for a family event that could be confirmed by bureaucrats, such as a wedding or a funeral. But systematic police checks of these documents had largely ended by 1997, with the exception of travelers bound for Pyongyang and other restricted areas.[1] The rules eased as famine drove people out on the roads in search of food. Since then, bribes from traders have kept police and other security officials from enforcing the law. Put bluntly, the greed of North Korea's cash-hungry cadre seemed to enable Shin's trek.

In all probability, the truck he rode in was a military vehicle that had been illegally converted into a for-profit people mover. The system, known as *servi-cha*, or service car, was invented in the late 1990s by government and military elites to milk cash from traders who needed to move themselves and their goods around the country. It was part of an upstart transportation system that the Daily NK, a Seoul-based Web site with informants in the North, describes as the country's "core transportation tool" and probably the "most decisive influence on the growth" of private markets.[2]

In North Korea, vehicles are owned not by individuals, but by the government, the party, and the military. Savvy operators within these organizations diverted trucks and colluded with smugglers to import fleets of secondhand cars, vans, and buses from China. After the vehi-cles were registered in the name of state entities, private drivers were hired, and wanderers like Shin were offered low-cost, no-questions-asked transport around much of the country.

Insurgent capitalism frightened the government of North Korea, which fretted publicly about a slippery slope to regime change and catastrophe. But periodic attempts to discipline bribe takers, restrict market activities, force *servi-cha* vehicles off the road, and confiscate cash were met with widespread resistance. Much of it came from poorly paid state functionaries whose livelihoods depended on using police and administrative authority to extract cash from upstart capitalists.

To force traders to pay, North Korean security forces invented a new twist on labor camps of the sort that Shin was born in. Instead of holding political criminals for life, these camps briefly incarcerated— and occasionally tortured—traders who failed to pay bribes to security officials. Officials periodically descended on the markets and arrested traders under vague laws that criminalize buying and selling. Traders avoided a grisly trip to a labor camp only by paying hard currency bribes.

The existence of these camps, which the government began to build before Shin's escape, was first disclosed in "Economic Crime and Punishment in North Korea," a report based on surveys of more than sixteen hundred refugees interviewed in China and South Korea between 2004 and 2008.

Security officials used the camps as "a system for shaking people down," Marcus Noland, a Washington-based economist and coauthor of the report, told me. "It really looks like the work of a gang, a kind of 'Soprano' state."

About two thirds of those held in these camps were allowed to go home within a month, according to the refugee survey. The compounds were often small, with few guards and not much fencing, but during their brief stays inside, many North Koreans said they routinely witnessed executions and deaths from torture and starvation. The effect of this revolving-door incarceration for economic crimes spread fear among people who made their living by trading.

"[The North Korean government] orders police to restrict the markets, but they don't always do what they are told because so many police and other authorities are making money," said Jiro Ishimaru, the editor of *Rimjin-gang*, a Japan-based journal that compiles eyewitness reports, photos, and videos smuggled out by anonymous reporters. "People on the outside don't realize it, but North Korea right now is in a drastic state of change."

Shin arrived at night near the train station in Hamhung, a coastal city of about three quarters of a million people. Most of them worked in factories, or did, before factories shut down owing to a lack of electricity and manufacturing supplies.

During the 1990s famine, the state distribution system utterly collapsed in Hamhung, leaving workers with no alternative sources of food. As a result, the city was hit harder by famine and starvation than any other population center in North Korea, according to refugee accounts.[3] Visiting Western journalists noticed in 1997 that hills surrounding the city were covered with fresh graves. One survivor said that ten percent of the city's population died, while another estimated that ten percent had fled the city in search of food.

In 2005, when Shin arrived in Hamhung, most of its factories were still closed. But the bulk of North Korea's north-south train traffic continued to pass through its rail yards.

Under cover of darkness, Shin went with other traders from the truck to a part of the rail yard where freight trains were assembled and dispatched. He saw a few guards around the station, but they were not checking IDs, and they made no effort to keep traders away from freight trains.

Still following other men, Shin climbed into a boxcar bound for

Chongjin, the largest city in the far north of the country and a gateway to rail lines leading to the Chinese border. The train pulled out before dawn on a journey of about 174 miles. If all went well, it would take a day, maybe two.

Shin soon learned what everyone else in North Korea had known for years—trains go slow, if they go at all.

Over the next three days, he traveled less than a hundred miles. In the boxcar, Shin befriended a young man of about twenty who said he was headed home to Gilju, a city of sixty-five thousand people on the main rail line to Chongjin. The man said he was returning from a failed attempt to find work; he had no food, no money, and no winter coat. But he offered to let Shin stay for a few days in his family's apartment, where he said it would be warm and where there was food to eat.

Shin needed rest. He was exhausted and starving. The food he had purchased in Bukchang was gone. The burns on his legs continued to bleed. He gratefully accepted the young man's offer.

It was early evening, cold, and beginning to snow when they got off the train at the Gilju station. At the suggestion of Shin's new friend, who knew cheap places to eat, they stopped on the way to his apartment and bought hot noodles from a street vendor. Shin paid for the meal with the last of the money he had received for his stolen rice.

When they finished their noodles, the young man said his family's apartment was just around the corner, but that he was embarrassed to greet his parents wearing threadbare clothes. He asked if Shin would mind lending him his coat for a few minutes. As soon as he had paid his respects to his family, the young man said, he would return to the noodle stand and take Shin up to the apartment, where they could get warm and sleep.

Since escaping the camp, Shin had been struggling to learn what normal behavior was for North Koreans. But after only a week, he had not figured out much. Lending a coat to a friend who needed to save face with his mother and father could be normal, Shin thought. He handed over the coat and agreed to wait.

Hours passed. Snow continued to fall. His friend did not return. Shin had not thought to follow him and see what apartment building he had disappeared into. Shin started to search nearby streets. He found no trace of him. After several hours of confused shivering, he wrapped himself in a dirty plastic tarp he found on the street and waited for morning.

For the next twenty days, Shin roamed around Gilju. With no coat, no money, no contacts, and no idea of where he should go, it was a formidable task simply to stay alive. The average January temperature in the city is 18 degrees Fahrenheit, well below freezing.

One thing saved him: the company—and larcenous advice—of the city's homeless, many of them teenagers. He found them around the train station, where they begged, gossiped, and periodically struck off in packs looking for food.

The crew Shin joined specialized in digging up daikon. It is a large, white, carrot-shaped East Asian radish that is often made into *kimchi*, the spicy fermented condiment that is Korea's most famous dish. To keep the fall crop of daikon from freezing during the cold months, North Koreans sometimes bury them in mounds.

During the day, Shin followed teams of teenage thieves to the outskirts of the city, looking for isolated houses with telltale mounds of dirt in their gardens. After a day of digging up and eating raw daikons, Shin returned to the city center with as many as he could carry, sold them in markets, and bought snacks. When he couldn't steal daikons, he scavenged through trash.

At night, Shin again followed the homeless to semisheltered sleeping places they had found near buildings with central heating systems. He also slept in haystacks and near open fires that the homeless would sometimes build.

He made no friends and was still careful not to talk about himself.

In Gilju, as across all of North Korea, Shin saw photographs of Kim Jong Il and Kim Il Sung everywhere—in train stations, town squares, and the homes he sometimes broke into. But no one, not even vagabonds and homeless teens, dared criticize or poke fun at their leaders. Surveys of recent defectors in China have found that this fear is persistent and almost universal.

For Shin, the biggest struggle remained finding enough to eat. But marauding for food was hardly an exceptional activity in North Korea.

"Stealing was always a problem," Charles Robert Jenkins wrote in his 2008 memoir about forty years of living inside the country. "If you didn't watch your things, someone would always be happy to relieve you of them."[4]

Jenkins was an ill-educated and deeply unhappy U.S. Army sergeant serving in South Korea in 1965, when he decided the grass would be greener in North Korea. He drank ten beers, stumbled across the world's most heavily militarized border, and surrendered his M14 rifle to startled North Korean soldiers.

"I was so ignorant," he told me. He said he had deserted the army for self-imposed incarceration in "a giant, demented prison."

Yet as an American deserter, Jenkins was much more than a prisoner. The North Korean government turned him into an actor who always played an evil Caucasian face in propaganda movies that demonized the United States.

Security officials also gave him a young Japanese woman and urged him to rape her. She had been abducted from her hometown in Japan on August 12, 1978, as part of a long-running and long-concealed North Korean operation that snatched young Japanese from coastal communities. Three North Korean agents grabbed her at dusk near a beach, stuffed her into a black body bag, and stole her away on a ship.

The woman, Hitomi Soga, ended up falling in love with Jenkins. They married and raised two daughters, both of whom were enrolled in a Pyongyang school that trained multilingual spies.

The beginning of the end of Jenkins's strange adventures in North Korea came when Japanese prime minister Junichiro Koizumi flew to Pyongyang for an extraordinary encounter with Kim Jong Il. During that 2002 meeting, Kim admitted to Koizumi that his agents had abducted thirteen Japanese civilians in the 1970s and 1980s, including Jenkins's wife Hitomi. She was immediately allowed to leave the country on Koizumi's airplane. After the Japanese prime minister made a second trip to North Korea in 2004, Jenkins and his daughters were also allowed to leave.

When I interviewed Jenkins, he and his family lived on Japan's remote Sado Island, where his wife was born and where North Korean agents had kidnapped her.

During his decades in the North, Jenkins had a house in the countryside and cultivated a large garden that helped feed his family. He also received a monthly cash payment from the government—enough to make sure that they did not starve during the famine. Still, he and his family had to fend off thieving neighbors and roaming soldiers in order to survive.

"It became routine for us as the corn ripened to pull all-night guard watches because the army would pick us clean," he wrote.

Thieving peaked during the 1990s famine, when gangs of homeless youngsters—many of them orphans—began to congregate around train stations in cities like Gilju, Hamhung, and Chongjin.

Their behavior and their desperation is described in *Nothing to Envy*, Barbara Demick's book about how ordinary North Koreans endured the famine years.

At Chongjin train station, she wrote, children snatched snacks out of travelers' hands. Working in teams, older ones knocked over food stands and tempted vendors to give chase. Then younger kids moved in to pick up spilled food. Children also used sharp sticks to poke holes in bags of grain on slow-moving trains and trucks.[5]

During the famine, train station cleaning staff made rounds with a wooden handcart, collecting bodies from the station floor, wrote Demick. There were widespread rumors of cannibalism, with claims that some children hanging around the station were drugged, killed, and butchered for meat.

Although the practice was not widespread, Demick concluded it did occur.

"From my interviews with defectors, it does appear that there were at least two cases . . . in which people were arrested and executed for cannibalism."

When Shin was stuck in Gilju in January 2005, the food situation was much less dire.

Harvests across North Korea had been relatively good in 2004. South Korea was pumping in food aid and free fertilizer. Food aid from China and the World Food Program was also flooding into state coffers—and some of it ended up in street markets.

The homeless around the train station were hungry, but Shin, in his time on the streets of Gilju, never saw anyone dying or dead from exposure or hunger.

Markets in the city were booming with abundant supplies of dried, fresh, and processed foods, including milled rice, tofu, crackers, cakes, and meat. Clothes, kitchenware, and electronics were also on sale. When Shin showed up with stolen daikon, he found market women eager to pay cash.

As he scrounged in Gilju, escape to China slipped from Shin's mind. The homeless whose ranks he had joined had other plans. They intended to travel in March to a state-owned farm to plant potatoes, a job that provided regular meals. With nothing else to do and no other contacts, Shin decided to tag along with them. His plan changed again, however, after one exceptionally productive day of thieving.

In the countryside on the outskirts of town, Shin wandered away from his crew, whose members were digging up a vegetable garden. By himself, he went around to the back of a vacant house and broke in through a window.

Inside, he found winter clothes, a military-style woolen hat, and a fifteen-pound bag of rice. He changed into the warmer clothes and carried the rice in his backpack to a Gilju merchant, who bought it for six thousand won, about six dollars.

With a new wad of cash for food and bribes, China again seemed possible. Shin walked to the freight yard at Gilju station and crawled aboard a northbound boxcar.

CHAPTER 18

THE BORDER

The Tumen River, which forms about a third of the border between North Korea and China, is shallow and narrow. It usually freezes over in winter, and walking across it takes only a few minutes. In most areas, the Chinese bank of the river offers decent cover; it is thick with trees. Chinese border guards are sparse.

Shin learned about the Tumen from traders on the train. But he did not have detailed information about where to cross it or what bribes would be acceptable to the North Korean guards who patrol along its southern bank.

So he traveled by boxcar from Gilju to Chongjin to Gomusan, a rail junction about twenty-five miles from the border, and began asking questions of local people.

"Hello, isn't it cold?" he said to an elderly man crouched on the steps of the Gomusan train station.

Shin offered crackers.

"Oh, thank you so much," the man said. "May I ask you where you are from?"

Shin had come up with a truthful but vague answer. He said he had run away from home in South Pyongan Province, where Camp 14 is located, because he was hungry and life was hard.

The old man said his life had been much easier when he lived in China, where food and work were easy to find. Eight months earlier, the man said, Chinese police had arrested him and sent him back to North Korea, where he had served a few months in a labor camp. He asked if Shin had considered going there.

"Can anyone cross over to China?" Shin said, trying to control his curiosity and his excitement.

The old man needed little prompting. He talked about China for more than half a day, explaining where to cross the Tumen and how to behave at the checkpoints near the border. Most of the guards, he said, were eager for bribes. His other instructions: When guards ask for identification, give them a few cigarettes and a package of crackers, along with small amounts of cash. Tell them you are a soldier. Tell them you are going to visit family members in China.

Early the next morning, Shin hopped a coal train bound for nearby Musan, a mining town on the border. He had been warned that the town was crawling with soldiers, so he jumped from the train as it slowed to enter Musan station and headed southwest on foot. He walked all day, about eighteen miles, looking for a stretch of the Tumen that was shallow and easily crossed.

With no identification papers, Shin knew he would be arrested if border guards did their job. At the first checkpoint, a guard asked for his papers. Trying to hide his fear, Shin said he was a soldier returning home. It helped that his clothing and his woolen hat, stolen back in Gilju, were the dark green of army uniforms.

"Here, smoke this," Shin said, handing the guard two packs of cigarettes.

The guard took the cigarettes and gestured for Shin to pass.

At a second checkpoint, another guard asked Shin for identification. Again he proffered cigarettes and a bag of crackers. Walking on, he met a third border guard and a fourth. They were young, scrawny, and hungry. Before Shin could say a word, they asked him for cigarettes and food—but not for identification.

Shin could not have escaped North Korea without an abundance of luck, especially at the border. As he bribed his way toward China in late January 2005, a window happened to be open, allowing relatively low-risk illegal passage across the border.

The North Korean government had been forced—by catastrophic famine in the mid-1990s and the importance of Chinese foodstuffs in feeding the population—to tolerate a porous border with China. That tolerance became semiofficial policy in 2000, when North Korea promised leniency to those who had fled the country in search of food. It was a belated admission that tens of thousands of famine-stricken North Koreans had already gone to China and that the country was increasingly dependent on their remittances. Also, by 2000, traders by the thousands had begun to move back and forth across the border supplying food and goods for markets that had all but replaced the government's public distribution system.

Following Kim's decree, arrested border crossers were released after a few days of questioning or, at most, a few months in labor camps, unless interrogators determined that they had had contact in China with South Koreans or missionaries.[1] The North Korean government also began to recognize and enable the role of traders in feeding the population. After six months of paperwork and a background check, government officials—especially if they received bribes—would sometimes issue certificates to traders that allowed them to cross back and forth into China legally.[2]

A porous border changed lives. Regular travelers to rural parts of North Korea noticed that far more people seemed to be wearing warm winter coats and that private markets were selling used Chinese television sets and video players, along with pirated video tapes and video CDs. (Video CDs offer much lower resolution than DVDs, but CD players were cheaper than DVD players and more affordable to North Koreans.)

North Korean defectors arriving in Seoul said that Chinese-made transistor radios had allowed them to listen to Chinese and South Korean stations, as well as to Radio Free Asia and Voice of America. Many told stories about how they had become addicted to Hollywood movies and South Korean soap operas.

"We closed the drapes and turned the volume down low whenever we watched the James Bond videos," a forty-year-old housewife from North Korea told me in Seoul. She fled her fishing village in a boat with her husband and son. "Those movies were how I started to learn what is going on in the world, how people learned the government of Kim Jong Il is not really for their own good."

Her son told me he fell in love with the United States, where he hoped to live one day, by watching blurry videos of *Charlie's Angels*.

As the trickle of foreign videos turned into a flood, North Korean police became alarmed and came up with new tactics to arrest people who watched them. They cut electricity to specific apartment blocks and then raided every apartment to see what tapes and disks were stuck inside the players.

Around the time that Shin and Park were formulating their escape plan, the North Korean government concluded that the border had become far too porous and posed a threat to internal security. Pyongyang was particularly enraged by South Korean and American initiatives that made it easier for North Korean defectors who had crossed into China to travel even farther, and settle in the West. In the summer of 2004, in the largest single mass defection, South Korea flew 468 North Koreans from Vietnam to Seoul. North Korea's news agency denounced the flight as "premeditated allurement, abduction, and terrorism." About the same time, Congress passed a law that accepted North Korean refugees for resettlement in the United States, which the North derided as an attempt to topple its government under the pretext of promoting democracy.

For these reasons, border rules began to change in late 2004. North Korea announced a new policy of harsh punishment for illegal border crossings, with prison terms of up to five years. In 2006, Amnesty International interviewed sixteen border crossers who said that the new rules were in effect, and that authorities in the North were circulating warnings that even first-time crossers would be sent to prison for at least a year. To enforce its rules, North Korea began a substantial buildup of electronic and photographic surveillance along the border. It extended barbed wire and built new concrete barriers.[3] China, too, increased border security to discourage North Koreans from entering the country in the run-up to the 2008 Summer Olympics.

At the end of January 2005, when Shin went walking toward China with cigarettes and snacks, the window on low-risk passage across the border was almost certainly beginning to close. But he was lucky: orders from on high had not yet changed the bribe-hungry behavior of the four bedraggled soldiers Shin met at guard stations along the Tumen River.

"I'm dying of hunger here," said the last soldier Shin bribed on his way out of North Korea. He looked to be about sixteen. "Don't you have anything to eat?"

His guard post was near a bridge that crossed into China. Shin gave him bean-curd sausage, cigarettes, and a bag of candy.

"Do a lot of people cross into China?" Shin asked.

"Or course," the guard replied. "They cross with the army's blessing and return after making good money."

In Camp 14, Shin had often discussed with Park what they would do after they crossed the border. They had planned to stay with Park's uncle, and that uncle now came into Shin's mind.

"Would it be possible for me to visit my uncle who lives in the village across the river?" Shin asked, although he had no idea where Park's uncle actually lived. "When I return, I'll treat you."

"Sure, go ahead," the guard replied. "But I am only on duty until seven tonight. So come back before then, all right?"

The guard led Shin through a forest to the river, where he said the crossing would be safe. It was late afternoon, but Shin promised to be back in plenty of time with food for the guard.

"Is the river frozen?" Shin asked. "Will I be okay?"

The guard assured him that the river was frozen, and that even if he broke through, the water was only ankle-deep.

"You should be fine," he said.

The river was about a hundred yards wide. Shin walked slowly out onto the ice. Halfway across, he broke through and icy water soaked his shoes. He jumped backward onto firm ice and crawled the rest of the way to China.

On the far bank, Shin stood up and turned around to take a last look at North Korea.

He wondered if his father had been killed back in the camp.

The young North Korean border guard had been watching Shin's progress. He flicked his wrist impatiently, gesturing for Shin to hurry up and disappear into the woods.

CHAPTER 19

CHINA

Shin scurried up the riverbank and hid briefly in the woods, where his wet feet began to freeze. It was getting dark and he was exhausted from a long day in the cold. Having reserved his limited cash for the cigarettes and snacks he gave to border guards, he had eaten little in recent days.

To warm up and get away from the river, he climbed a hill and followed a road through fields blanketed in snow. In the near distance, beyond the fields, he could see a cluster of houses.

Between Shin and the houses, there were two men on the road. They had flashlights and wore vests that had Chinese lettering printed across the back. He later learned they were Chinese border patrol soldiers. Since 2002, when hundreds of North Korean asylum seekers embarrassed China by rushing into foreign embassies, soldiers had begun rounding up illegal border crossers and forcibly repatriating tens of thousands of them.[1] The soldiers Shin saw were gazing up at the sky. He guessed they were counting stars. In any case, Shin's presence did not seem to interest them. He hurried on toward the houses.

His plan for surviving in China was as half-baked as his plan had been for escaping North Korea. He did not know where to go or whom to contact. He simply wanted to get as far from the border as possible. He had walked into a poor, mountainous, and sparsely populated part of China's Jilin Province. The nearest town of any size was Helong, about thirty miles north of where he crossed the river. His one hope was the gossip he had picked up from itinerant traders in North Korea: ethnic Koreans living in the Chinese border region might be willing to offer him shelter and food—and maybe a job.

Entering a yard outside one of the houses, Shin set off a mad eruption of barking dogs. He counted seven of them—an eyebrow-raising number by the standards of North Korea, where the pet population had been culled by scavengers, many of them orphans, who stole, skinned, and barbecued dogs during the famine years.[2]

When the front door opened, Shin pleaded for something to eat and a place to sleep. A Korean Chinese man told him to go away. He said police had warned him that very morning not to help North Koreans. Shin moved on to a nearby brick house, where he asked another Korean Chinese man for help. Again, he was told to move on. This time, rudely.

Shin was desperately cold as he left the yard. He saw the remains of a fire in an outdoor cooking pit. After digging out three smoldering logs, he carried them into a nearby larch forest, scraped away the snow from the ground, found some kindling, and managed to start a campfire. He took off his wet shoes and socks so they could dry near the fire. Without intending to, he fell asleep.

At dawn, the fire was dead. Shin's face was covered in frost. Cold to the bone, he put on his shoes and socks, which were still wet. He walked all morning, following back roads he hoped led away from the border. Around noon, he saw a police checkpoint in the distance, left the road, found another house, and knocked on the door.

"Could I get some help, please?" he begged.

A Korean Chinese man refused to let him in the house. He said his wife was mentally ill. But he gave Shin two apples.

To avoid checkpoints and get farther away from the border, Shin followed a winding footpath up into the mountains, where he walked for most of the day. (Shin is not sure where he walked that first day in China; Google Earth images of the region near the border show forested mountains and a few scattered houses.) At dusk, he tried another farmhouse, newly built of cinder blocks and surrounded by pigpens. Five dogs barked as he entered the yard.

A middle-aged man poked his pudgy face out the front door.

"Are you from North Korea?" the man asked.

Shin nodded wearily.

The man, a Chinese farmer who spoke some Korean, invited Shin inside and ordered a young woman to cook rice. The farmer said he had once employed two North Korean defectors and that they had been useful workers. He offered Shin food, lodging, and five yuan a day—about sixty cents—if he was willing to tend pigs.

Before he had eaten his first hot meal in China, Shin had a job and a place to sleep. He had been a prisoner, a snitch, a fugitive, and a thief, but never an employee. The job was an opportune beginning and a colossal relief. It ended a fearful, freezing month on the run. A lifetime of slavery shifted suddenly into the past tense.

In the pig farmer's kitchen over the next month, Shin finally found plenty to eat. He filled his stomach three times a day with the roasted meat that he and Park had fantasized about in Camp 14. He bathed with soap and hot water. He got rid of the lice he had lived with since birth.

The farmer bought Shin antibiotics for the burns on his legs, along with warm winter clothes and work boots. Shin threw away the stolen, ill-fitting clothes that identified him as a North Korean.

He had a room of his own, where he slept on the floor with several blankets. He was able to sleep as much as ten hours a night, an unimaginable luxury. The young woman in the house—Shin found out she was the farmer's mistress—cooked for him and taught him rudimentary Chinese.

He worked from dawn until seven or eight at night for his sixty cents a day. Besides tending pigs, he hunted with the farmer for wild boar in the surrounding mountains. After the farmer shot them, Shin lugged their carcasses out of the woods for slaughter and commercial sale.

While the work was often exhausting, no one slapped, kicked, or punched Shin, and no one threatened him. Fear began to ebb away as abundant food and sleep made it possible for him to regain his strength. When police visited the farm, the farmer told Shin to pretend to be a mute. The farmer vouched for his good character, and the police went away.

Still, Shin understood that he was only welcome in the farmer's house because he was cheap labor.

The capacity of the Chinese borderlands to absorb North Koreans is significant—and significantly underappreciated outside of Northeast Asia. The area is not all that foreign—or unwelcoming—to Korean-speaking migrants.

When defectors cross into China, the first "foreigners" they encounter are usually ethnic Koreans who speak the same language, eat similar food, and share some of the same cultural values. With a bit of luck, they can, like Shin, find work, shelter, and a measure of safety.

This has been going on since the late 1860s, when famine struck North Korea and starving farmers fled across the Tumen and the Yalu rivers into northeast China. Later, China's imperial government recruited Korean farmers to create a buffer against Russian expansion, and Korea's Choson Dynasty allowed them to depart legally. Before World War II, the Japanese who occupied the Korean Peninsula and northeast China pushed tens of thousands of Korean farmers across the border to weaken China's hold on the region.

Nearly two million ethnic Koreans now live in China's three northeast provinces, with the highest concentration in Jilin, which Shin entered when he crawled across the frozen river. Inside Jilin Province, China created the Yanbian Korean Autonomous Prefecture, where forty percent of the population is ethnic Korean and where the government subsidizes Korean-language schools and publications.

Korean speakers living in northeast China have also been an unsung force for cultural change inside North Korea. They have affected this change by watching South Korean soap operas on home satellite dishes, recording low-quality video CDs, and smuggling hundreds of thousands of them across the border into North Korea, where they sell for as little as fifteen cents, according to *Rimjin-gang*, the Osaka-based magazine that has informants based in the North.

South Korean soaps—which display the fast cars, opulent houses, and surging confidence of South Korea—are classified as "impure recorded visual materials" and are illegal to watch in North Korea. But they have developed a huge following in Pyongyang and other cities, where police officers assigned to confiscate the videos are reportedly watching them and where teenagers imitate the silky intonations of the Korean language as it is spoken by upper-crust stars in Seoul.[3]

These TV programs have demolished decades of North Korean propaganda, which claims that the South is a poor, repressed, and unhappy place, and that South Koreans long for unification under the fatherly hand of the Kim dynasty.

In the past half century, the governments of China and North Korea have cooperatively used their security forces to make sure that the intermittent seepage of Koreans across the border never turns into a flood. A secret agreement on border security was signed between the two countries in the early 1960s, according to the South Korean government. A second agreement in 1986 committed China to sending North Korean defectors back home, where they often face arrest, torture, and months or years of forced labor.

By imprisoning its citizens inside the country, North Korea defies an international agreement that it has pledged to uphold. The 1966 agreement says: "Everyone shall be free to leave any country, including his own."[4]

By defining all North Korean defectors as "economic refugees" and sending them home to be persecuted, China defies its obligations as a signatory to a 1951 international refugee convention. Beijing refuses to allow defectors to make claims for asylum and prevents the office of the U.N. High Commissioner for Refugees from working along the border with North Korea.

International law, in effect, has been trumped by the strategic interests of North Korea and China. A mass exodus from North Korea could substantially depopulate the country, undermine its already inadequate capacity to grow food, and weaken—or perhaps even topple—the government. The risk of such an exodus increases as China's economy soars, North Korea's sinks, and word spreads that life is better in China.

For the Chinese government, an uncontrolled surge of impoverished Korean refugees is undesirable for several reasons. It would dramatically worsen poverty in China's three northeast provinces, which have largely missed out on the wealth generated by the country's economic boom. More important, it might precipitate regime collapse in North Korea and lead to the unification of the Korean Peninsula under a Seoul-based government closely allied with the United States. In the process, China would lose a key buffer between one of its poorest regions and a united, affluent, and West-oriented Korea. That, in turn, could arouse nationalist sentiments among ethnic Koreans in the Chinese borderlands.

Beijing's distaste for North Korean defectors, as enforced by police and border soldiers, is well understood by farmers, factory foremen, and other bosses in China's northeast provinces.

But, as Shin found out, they are quite willing to ignore national directives when presented with an industrious North Korean who keeps his mouth shut and works hard for sixty cents a day. Chinese employers are also free to cheat, abuse, or get rid of their North Korean help at any time.

Within a month, Shin's arrangement with the farmer turned sour.

He was fetching water from a brook near the farm when he met two other North Korean defectors. They were hungry and cold and living in an abandoned shack in the woods not far from the pig farm. Shin asked the Chinese farmer to help them out, and he did so, but with a reluctance and a resentment that Shin was slow to notice.

One of the defectors was a woman in her forties who had crossed the border before. She had an estranged Chinese husband and a child. They lived nearby, and she wanted to contact them by phone. The farmer allowed her to use his telephone. Within a few days, she and the other defector were gone.

But giving shelter to three North Koreans had annoyed the farmer. He told Shin that he, too, would have to go.

The farmer knew of another job: tending livestock up in the mountains. He offered to drive Shin there in his car. After driving on mountain roads for two hours, the farmer dropped Shin off at a friend's cattle ranch. It was not far from Helong, a city of about eighty-five thousand people. If Shin worked hard, the farmer told him, he would be generously compensated.

Only when the farmer drove away did Shin discover that no one on the ranch spoke Korean.

CHAPTER 20
ASYLUM

For the next ten months, Shin stayed where the pig farmer had left him, tending cattle in mountain pastures and sleeping on a ranch-house floor with two surly Chinese cowhands. He was free to leave whenever he wanted. But he did not know where to go or what else to do.

The future was to have been Park's responsibility. Back in Camp 14, Park had assured Shin that once they made it to China he would arrange for passage to South Korea. Park would enlist the help of his uncle in China. They would be provided with money, paperwork, and contacts. But Park was dead and South Korea seemed impossibly far away.

Staying put, though, had some benefits. Shin's legs healed; scar tissue finally covered the electricity burns. From the cowherds and ranch manager he learned some conversational Chinese. And for the first time in his life he had access to an electric dream-making machine.

A radio.

Shin fiddled with its dial nearly every morning, switching among the dozen or so Korean-language stations that broadcast daily into North Korea and northeast China. These stations, with funding from

South Korea, the United States, and Japan, mix Asian and world news with sharply critical coverage of North Korea and the Kim dynasty. They focus on the North's chronic food shortages, human rights violations, military provocations, nuclear program, and dependence on China. Considerable airtime is devoted to the comfortable lives, by North Korean standards, of defectors living in South Korea, where they receive housing and other subsidies from the government in Seoul.

Defectors run some of these stations (with financial assistance from the United States and other sources) and they have recruited reporters inside North Korea. These reporters, who use cell phones and smuggle out sound and video recordings on tiny USB memory sticks, have revolutionized news coverage of North Korea. It took months for the outside world to learn of economic reforms that eased restrictions on private markets in North Korea in 2002. Seven years later, when the North Korean government launched a disastrous currency reform that impoverished and enraged tens of thousands of traders, the news was reported within hours by Free North Korea Radio.

Inside North Korea, the penalty for listening to these stations can be ten years in a labor camp. But the country has been flooded in recent years with three-dollar radios smuggled in from China, and between five and twenty percent of North Koreans are tuning in daily, according to survey research gathered in China from defectors, traders, and other border crossers.[1] Many of them have told researchers that listening to foreign radio provided an important motivation for leaving the country.[2]

Listening on the Chinese cattle ranch, Shin was comforted to hear voices speaking a language he understood. He heard the thrilling albeit year-old news that several hundred North Korean defectors had been flown from Vietnam to Seoul. He paid particularly close attention to reports about border-crossing conditions, the routes defectors were taking to travel from China to South Korea, and the lives they led after getting there.

Shin struggled, though, to make sense of most of what he heard on the radio.

The broadcasts were targeted at educated North Koreans, who had grown up with state media that venerates the godlike powers and wisdom of the Kim family dynasty and also warns that Americans, South Koreans, and Japanese are scheming to take over the entire Korean Peninsula. Camp 14 had cut Shin out of this propaganda loop, and he listened to the West's counterpropaganda with the ears of a child—curious, confused, sometimes even bored, but always lacking in context.

Park, during the four weeks he had lectured Shin on how the world worked, had also been sharply critical of the North Korean government. But Shin had only pretended to be interested, except when Park talked about food.

Shin was bewildered by much of the reporting about North Korea on the radio. He knew little about the Kim family and even less about how it was viewed around the world. Even when he heard juicy tidbits about the lives of defectors in China and South Korea, there was no one to share it with.

Without a common language to communicate with anyone, his loneliness on the cattle ranch became greater than it had been in the labor camp.

In late 2005, with winter rolling into the mountains, Shin decided to make his move.

He had heard on the radio that Korean churches in China sometimes helped defectors. So he came up with a sketchy plan: he would travel west and south, putting as much distance as possible between himself, North Korea, and border patrol soldiers. Then he would seek out friendly Koreans. With their help, he hoped to find a stable job in southern China and build a low-profile life. He had given up all hope of reaching South Korea.

Shin knew enough Chinese by then to tell the manager of the cattle ranch why he was leaving. He explained that if he continued to live near the border, he would be arrested by the police and forcibly sent back to North Korea.

Without saying much, the manager paid him six hundred yuan, or about seventy-two dollars. For the ten months he had tended cattle, it amounted to less than twenty-five cents a day. Based on the sixty cents a day he had earned at the pig farm, Shin's expectation was that he'd be paid at least twice as much.

He had been cheated, but like all North Koreans working in China he was in no position to protest. As a going-away present, the ranch manager gave Shin a map and took him to the bus station in nearby Helong.

Compared to traveling in North Korea, Shin found it easy and safe to travel in China. His clothing—the gift of the pig farmer—was made locally and attracted little attention. Traveling alone and keeping his mouth shut, he discovered that his face and his manner did not advertise his identity as a North Korean on the run.

Even when Shin mentioned that he had come from North Korea in conversation with ethnic Koreans he appealed to for food, cash, or work, he learned that he was nobody special. A long line of defectors had come begging ahead of him. Most of the people he encountered were not alarmed by or interested in North Koreans. They were sick of them.

No one asked to see Shin's identification papers when he bought a ticket in Helong for the 105-mile bus ride to Changchun, the capital of Jilin Province, or when he boarded a train for the 500-mile journey to

Beijing, or when he traveled more than 1,000 miles by bus to Chengdu, a city of five million people in southwest China.

Shin started to look for work when he arrived in Chengdu, a destination he had picked randomly at the bus station in Beijing.

At a Korean restaurant, he found a magazine that listed the names and addresses of several small churches. At each church, he asked to speak to the pastor, explaining that he was a North Korean in need of help. Ethnic Korean pastors gave him cash, as much as fifteen dollars' worth of yuan. But none offered work or lodging. They also told him to go away. It was illegal, they said, to help a defector.

When asking for help in China, Shin was careful not to say too much. He told no one that he was an escapee from a political labor camp, fearing that it might tempt someone to turn him over to the police. He tried to avoid long conversations. He also stayed away from hotels and guesthouses, where he feared he would be asked to show identification.

Instead, he spent many of his nights in PC bangs, the ubiquitous East Asian Internet cafés where young, mostly unmarried, men play computer games and surf the Internet around the clock.

Shin found he could get directions and some rest at a PC bang, if not exactly sleep. He looked like many of the aimless, unemployed young men who hang out in such places, and no one asked him for papers.

After eight churches turned him away in Chengdu, Shin made the long, miserable bus trip back to Beijing, where for ten days he refocused his job search on Korean restaurants. Sometimes the owners or managers would feed him or give him a bit of money. But none offered a job.

As he failed to find work, Shin did not panic or get discouraged. Food meant a lot more to him than it means to most people, and everywhere he went in China there was an impressive abundance of it. To his amazement, China was a place where even dogs seemed well fed, and if he ran low on cash to buy food, he begged. He found that Chinese people would usually give him something.

Shin came to believe that he would never starve. That alone calmed his nerves and gave him hope. He did not have to break into houses to find food, money, or clothing.

Shin left Beijing and took a 70-mile bus ride to Tianjin, a city of ten million people, where he tried again with Korean churches. Pastors again offered petty cash but no work or lodging. He took a bus about 220 miles south to Jinan, a city of five million, and spent five days searching out more Korean churches. Still, no work.

Again, he moved south. On February 6, 2006—a year and a week after he'd crossed the frozen Tumen River into China—Shin arrived in Hangzhou, a city of about six million in the Yangtze River Delta. At the third Korean restaurant he walked into, the owner offered him a job.

The restaurant, called Haedanghwa Korean Cuisine, was hectic and Shin worked long hours, washing dishes and cleaning tables. After eleven days, he had had enough. He told the owner he was quitting, collected his pay, and boarded a bus bound for Shanghai, about ninety miles to the south.

At a Shanghai bus station, Shin browsed through a Korean-language magazine, found a list of Korean restaurants, and went off again in search of work.

"May I meet the owner of this place?" Shin asked a waitress in the first restaurant on his list.

"Why do you ask?" the waitress replied.

"I am from North Korea, I just got off the bus, and I have no place to go," Shin said. "I was wondering if I could work in this restaurant."

The waitress said the owner was not available.

"Is there anything I can do here?" Shin begged.

"There are no jobs, but that man eating over there says he's from Korea, so you should ask him."

The waitress pointed to a customer eating a late lunch.

"Excuse me, I am from North Korea, looking for a job," Shin said. "Please help me."

After studying Shin's face for a while, the man asked him where his hometown was. Shin said he was from Bukchang, the town near Camp 14, the place where he had stolen his first bag of rice.

"Are you really from North Korea?" the man asked, pulling out a reporter's notebook and beginning to scribble notes.

Shin had stumbled upon a journalist, a Shanghai-based correspondent for a major South Korean media company.

"Why did you come to Shanghai?" he asked Shin.

Shin repeated what he had just said. He was looking for work. He was hungry. The journalist wrote everything down. This was not the kind of conversation Shin was used to. He had never met a journalist. It made him anxious.

After a long silence, the man asked Shin if he wanted to go to South Korea—a question that made Shin even more anxious. By the time Shin got to Shanghai, he had long since abandoned any hope of traveling to South Korea. He told the journalist he could not go there because he had no money.

The man suggested that they leave the restaurant together. Outside on the street, he stopped a cab, told Shin to get in, and climbed in beside him. After several minutes, he told Shin they were going to the South Korean Consulate.

Shin's growing unease turned to panic when the journalist went on to explain that there could be danger when they got out of the taxi. He told Shin that if anyone grabbed him, he should shake him off and run.

As they neared the consulate, they saw police cars and several uniformed officers milling around its entrance. Since 2002, the Beijing government had been attempting—with considerable success—to stop North Koreans from rushing into foreign embassies and consulates to seek asylum.

Shin had stayed away from the Chinese police. Fearing arrest and deportation, he had never dared break into houses for clothes or food. He had tried to be invisible, and he had succeeded.

Now a stranger was taking him into a heavily guarded building—and advising him to run if police tried to apprehend him.

When the taxi stopped in front of the building flying the South Korean flag, Shin's chest felt heavy. Out on the street, he feared he would not be able to walk. The journalist told him to smile; he put his arm around Shin and pulled him close to his body. Together they walked toward the consulate gate. Speaking in Chinese, the journalist told police that he and his friend had business inside.

Police opened the gate and waved them through.

Once they were inside, the journalist told Shin to relax. But Shin did not understand that he was safe. Despite repeated assurances from consulate staff, he could not believe he was really under the protection of the South Korean government. Diplomatic immunity did not make sense to him.

The consulate was comfortable, South Korean officials were helpful, and there was another North Korean defector inside the consulate to talk to.

For the first time in his life, Shin showered daily. He had new clothes, fresh underwear. Rested, scrubbed, and feeling increasingly safe, Shin waited for paperwork to be processed that would allow him to travel to South Korea.

He heard from officials in the consulate that the journalist who had helped him (and who still does not want his name or news organization made public) had gotten into trouble with Chinese authorities.

Then, after six months inside the consulate, Shin flew to Seoul, where the South Korean National Intelligence Service took an uncommon interest in him. During interrogation that lasted an entire month, Shin told NIS agents his life story. He tried to be as truthful as possible, while leaving out the part about snitching on his mother and brother.

CHAPTER 21

K'UREDIT K'ADUS

When intelligence agents were finished with Shin, he reported to Hanawon, which means "House of Unity" in Korean. It is a government-run resettlement center perched in verdant hill country about forty miles south of Seoul, a sprawling megalopolis of more than twenty million people The complex looks like a well-funded, security-obsessed mental hospital: three-story redbrick buildings encircled by a high fence surmounted by video cameras and patrolled by armed guards.

Hanawon was built in 1999 by the Ministry of Unification to house, feed, and teach North Korean defectors how to adjust and survive in the South's ultracompetitive capitalist culture.

To that end, the center has a staff that includes psychologists, career counselors, and teachers of everything from world history to driver's education. There are also doctors, nurses, and dentists. Over a three-month stay, defectors learn their rights under South Korean law and go on field trips to shopping centers, banks, and subway stations.

"Everyone who defects has adjustment problems," Ko Gyoung-bin, the director-general of Hanawon, told me when I visited the place.

Initially, Shin seemed to be adjusting better than most.

Field trips did not surprise or frighten him. Having navigated on his own through several of China's largest and most prosperous cities, he was accustomed to pushy crowds, tall buildings, flashy cars, and electronic gadgets.

During his first month at Hanawon, he received documents and photo identification that certified his South Korea citizenship, which the government automatically bestows on all those who flee the North. He also attended classes that explained the many government benefits and programs offered to defectors, including a free apartment, an eight-hundred-dollar-a-month settlement stipend for two years, and as much as eighteen thousand dollars if he stuck with job training or higher education.

In a classroom with other defectors, he learned that the Korean War started when North Korea launched an unprovoked surprise invasion of the South on June 25, 1950. It's a history lesson that flabbergasts most newcomers from the North. Beginning in early childhood, their government has taught them that South Korea started the war with the encouragement and armed assistance of the United States. At Hanawon, many defectors flatly refuse to believe that this fundamental pillar of North Korean history is a lie. They become angry. It is a reaction comparable to the way Americans might respond to someone who told them that World War II started in the Pacific after an American sneak attack on Tokyo harbor.

Since Shin had been taught next to nothing in Camp 14, a radically revised history of the Korean Peninsula was not meaningful to him. He was far more interested in classes that taught him how to use a computer and find information on the Internet.

Toward the end of his first month at Hanawon, just as he had begun to get comfortable in the place, Shin started to have disturbing dreams. He saw his mother hanged, Park's body on the fence, and visualized the torture he believed his father was subjected to after his escape. As the nightmares continued, he dropped out of a course in automobile repair. He did not take driver's ed. He stopped eating. He struggled to sleep. He was all but paralyzed by guilt.

Nearly all defectors arrive at Hanawon showing clinical symptoms of paranoia. They whisper and get in fistfights. They are afraid to disclose their names, ages, or place of birth. Their manners often offend South Koreans. They tend not to say "thank you" or "sorry."

Questions from South Korean bank tellers, whom they meet on field trips to open bank accounts, often terrify defectors. They doubt the motives of nearly all people in positions of authority. They feel guilty about those they left behind. They fret, sometimes to the point of panic, about their educational and financial inferiority to South Koreans. They are ashamed of the way they dress, talk, and even wear their hair.

"In North Korea, paranoia was a rational response to real conditions and it helped these people survive," said Kim Hee-kyung, a clinical psychologist who spoke to me in her office at Hanawon. "But it keeps them from understanding what is going on in South Korea. It is a real obstacle to assimilation."

Teenagers from the North spend two months to two years at Hangyoreh Middle-High School, a government-funded remedial boarding school affiliated with Hanawon. It was built in 2006 to help newly arrived youngsters from the North, most of whom are unfit for public school in South Korea.

Nearly all of them struggle with basic reading and math. Some are cognitively impaired, apparently from acute malnourishment as infants. Even among the brightest youngsters, their knowledge of world history essentially comprises the mythical personal stories of their Great Leader, Kim Il Sung, and his dear son, Kim Jong Il.

"Education in North Korea is useless for life in South Korea," Gwak

Jong-moon, principal of Hangyoreh, told me. "When you are too hungry, you don't go to learn and teachers don't go to teach. Many of our students have been hiding in China for years with no access to schools. As young children in North Korea, they grew up eating bark off trees and thinking it was normal."

During field trips to the movies, young defectors often panic when lights go down, afraid that someone might kidnap them. They are bewildered by Korean as spoken in South Korea, where the language has been infected with Americanisms such as *syop'ing* (shopping) and *k'akt'eil* (cocktail).

They find it incredible that money is stored in plastic *k'uredit k'adus*.

Pizza, hot dogs, and hamburgers—staples of South Korean teen cuisine—give them indigestion. So does too much rice, the one-time staple that in the postfamine era has become a food for the rich in North Korea.

One teenage girl at Hangyoreh School gargled with liquid fabric softener, mistaking it for mouthwash. Another used laundry detergent as baking flour. Many are terrified when they first hear the noise of an electric washing machine.

In addition to being paranoid, confused, and intermittently technophobic, defectors tend to suffer from preventable diseases and conditions that are all but nonexistent in South Korea. The head nurse at Hanawon for the past decade, Chun Jung-hee, told me that a high percentage of women from the North have chronic gynecological infections and cysts. She said many defectors arrive infected with tuberculosis that has never been treated with antibiotics. They also commonly arrive with chronic indigestion and hepatitis B. Routine medical ailments are often difficult to diagnose, the nurse said, because defectors are unaccustomed to and suspicious of doctors who ask them personal questions and prescribe medications. Men, women, and children have serious dental problems resulting from malnutrition and a lack of calcium in their diets. Half the money spent annually on medical care at Hanawon goes for prosthetic dental treatment.

Many, if not most, defectors arriving at Hanawon escaped North Korea with the help of brokers based in South Korea. The brokers wait eagerly for defectors to graduate from the settlement center and begin receiving monthly stipends from the government. Then they demand their money. Anxiety about debt torments defectors inside Hanawon, the head nurse told me.

Shin did not have to worry about brokers, and his physical health was relatively good after a half year of rest and regular meals in the consulate in Shanghai.

But his nightmares would not go away.

They became more frequent and more upsetting. He found his comfortable, well-nourished life impossible to reconcile with the grisly images from Camp 14 that played inside his head.

As his mental health deteriorated, Hanawon's medical staff realized he needed special care and transferred him to the psychiatric ward of a nearby hospital, where he spent two and a half months, some of it in isolation, and most of it on medication that allowed him to sleep and eat.

He had started keeping a diary in the South Korean Consulate in Shanghai, and doctors in the hospital's psychiatric ward encouraged him to keep writing in it as part of his treatment for what they diagnosed as post-traumatic stress disorder.

Shin remembers little of his time in the hospital, except that the nightmares slowly diminished.

After his discharge, he moved into a small apartment purchased for him by the Ministry of Unification. It was located in Hwaseong, a city of about five hundred thousand people in the low plains of the central Korean Peninsula, near the Yellow Sea. Hwaseong is about thirty miles south of Seoul.

For the first month, Shin rarely went outdoors. He watched South Korean life unfold from the windows of his apartment. Eventually, he ventured out to the streets. Shin compares his emergence to the slow growth of a fingernail. He cannot explain how it happened or why. It just did.

After he began to venture into the city, he took driving lessons. Owing to his limited vocabulary, he twice flunked the written driver's license test. Shin found it difficult to find a job that interested him or hold a job he was offered. He collected scrap metal, made clay pots, and worked in a convenience store.

Career counselors at Hanawon say most North Koreans have similar experiences of exile. They often depend on the South Korean government to solve their problems, and fail to take personal responsibility for poor work habits or for showing up late on the job. Defectors frequently quit jobs found for them by the government and start businesses that fail. Some newcomers are disgusted by what they see as the decadence and inequality of life in the South. To find employers who will put up with the prickliness of newcomers from the North, the Ministry of Unification pays companies up to eighteen hundred dollars a year if they risk hiring a defector.

Shin spent long hours by himself, feeling desperately lonely, in his one-room apartment. He tried to locate his oldest uncle, Shin Tae Sub— whose flight to South Korea after the Korean War was the crime for which Shin's father and his entire family had been sent to Camp 14.

But Shin had only a name, and the South Korean government told him it had no information on that name. The Unification Ministry said it could search only for people who had registered to be reunited with lost family members. Shin gave up the search.

One of the psychiatrists who had treated Shin in the hospital connected him with a counselor from the Database Center for North Korean Human Rights, a nongovernment organization in Seoul that gathers, analyzes, and publishes information about abuses in the North.

The counselor encouraged Shin to turn his therapeutic dairy into the memoir that the Database Center published in Korean in 2007. While working on the book, Shin began spending nearly all his time at the office of the Database Center in Seoul, where he was given a place to sleep, and made friends with his editors and other staff.

As word spread in Seoul of his birth in and escape from a no-exit labor camp, he began to meet many of the South's leading human rights activists and heads of defector organizations. His story was vetted and scrutinized by former prisoners and guards from the camps, as well as by human rights lawyers, South Korean journalists, and other experts with extensive knowledge of the camps. His understanding of how the camps operate, his scarred body, and the haunted look in his eyes were persuasive—and he was widely acknowledged as the first North Korean to come south after escaping from a political prison.

An Myeong Chul, the guard and driver at four camps in the North, told the *International Herald Tribune* that he had no doubt Shin had lived in a complete control zone. When they met, An said he noticed telltale signs: avoidance of eye contact and arms bowed by childhood labor.[1]

"At first, I could not believe Shin because no one ever before succeeded in the escape," Kim Tae Jin told me in 2008.[2] He is president of the Democracy Network Against North Korean Gulag and a defector who spent a decade in Camp 15 before he was released.

But Kim, like others with firsthand knowledge of the camps, concluded after meeting Shin that his story was as solid as it was extraordinary.

Outside South Korea, specialists in human rights began to take note of Shin. He was invited in the spring of 2008 to tour Japan and the United States. He appeared at the University of California, Berkeley, and Columbia University, and spoke to employees at Google.

As he made friends among people who understood and appreciated what he had endured, he gained confidence and began to try to fill gaping holes in his understanding of his homeland. He devoured news about North Korea, on the Internet and in South Korean newspapers. He read about the history of the Korean Peninsula, the reputation of the Kim family dictatorship, and his country's status as an international pariah.

At the Database Center, where staff members had been working with North Koreans for years, Shin was viewed as a kind of rough-hewn prodigy.

"Compared to other defectors, he was a fast learner and highly adaptable to culture shock," said Lee Yong-koo, a team leader there.

Tagging along with his new friends, Shin began going to church on Sunday mornings, but he did not understand the concept of a loving and forgiving God.

As a matter of instinct, Shin was reluctant to ask for anything. The teachers in the labor camp had punished children who asked questions. In Seoul, even when he was surrounded by solicitous and well-informed friends, Shin found it all but impossible to ask for help. He read voraciously, but would not use a dictionary to look up words he did not know. He would never ask a friend to explain something he did not understand. Because he blinkered out what he could not immediately comprehend, his travels to Tokyo, New York, and California did little to awaken a sense of wonder and excitement. Shin knew he was undermining his ability to adapt to his new life, but he also knew that he could not force himself to change.

CHAPTER 22

SOUTH KOREANS ARE NOT SO INTERESTED

The only birthdays that mattered in Camp 14 were those of Kim Jong Il and Kim Il Sung. They are national holidays in North Korea, and even in a no-exit labor camp, prisoners get the day off.

As for Shin's birthday, no one paid any attention when he was growing up, including Shin.

That changed when he turned twenty-six in South Korea. Four of his friends threw him a surprise party at T.G.I. Friday's in downtown Seoul.

"I was very moved," he told me when we met for the first time in December 2008, a few days after his birthday.

But such occasions were rare, and the birthday party notwithstanding, Shin was not happy in South Korea. He had recently quit a part-time job serving beer in a Seoul pub. He did not know how he would pay the rent on a tiny three-hundred-dollar-a-month room he occupied in a group apartment downtown and his monthly stipend of eight hundred dollars from the Ministry of Unification had run out. He had emptied his bank account. He worried out loud that he might have to join the homeless at the central train station in Seoul.

Nor was his social life in great shape. He shared the occasional meal with roommates in his group apartment, but he did not have a girlfriend or a best friend. He declined to socialize or work with other North Koreans who had been released from labor camps. In this respect, he was like many North Korean defectors. Studies have found that they are slow to socialize and often avoid contact with others for two to three years after arriving in the South.[1]

His memoir had flopped, about five hundred copies sold from a printing of three thousand. Shin said he made no money from the book.

"People are not so interested," Kim Sang-hun, the director of the Database Center, told the *Christian Science Monitor* after his organization published the book. "The indifference of South Korean society to the issue of North Korean rights is so awful."[2]

But Shin was by no means the first camp survivor from the North to be greeted with a collective yawn by the South Korean public.

Kang Chol-hwan spent a decade with his family in Camp 15 before they were pronounced "redeemable" and released in 1987. But his wrenching story, written with journalist Pierre Rigoulot and first published in French in 2000, also received scant attention in South Korea until after it had been translated into English as *The Aquariums of Pyongyang* and a copy found its way to the desk of President George W. Bush. He invited Kang to the White House to discuss North Korea, and later described *Aquariums* as "one of the most influential books I read during my presidency."[3]

"I don't want to be critical of this country," Shin told me the first day we met, "but I would say that out of the total population of South Korea, only .001 percent has any real interest in North Korea. Their ways of living do not allow them to think about things beyond their borders. There is nothing in it for them."

Shin exaggerated the South's lack of concern about the North, but he had a valid point. It's a blind spot that baffles local and international human rights groups. Overwhelming evidence of continuing atrocities inside the North's labor camps has done little to rouse the South Korean public. As the Korean Bar Association has noted, "South Koreans, who publicly cherish the virtue of brotherly love, have been inexplicably stuck in a deep quagmire of indifference."[4]

When South Korean president Lee Myung-bak was elected in 2007, just three percent of voters named North Korea as a primary concern. They told pollsters that their primary interest was in making higher salaries.

When it comes to making money, North Korea is an utter waste of time. South Korea's economy is 38 times larger than the North's; its international trade volume is 224 times larger.[5]

North Korea's periodic belligerence, however, does trigger eruptions of anger in the South. This was especially true in 2010, when North Korea launched a sneak submarine attack that killed forty-six South Korean sailors and sank the *Cheonan*, a warship sailing in South Korean territorial waters. The North also rained artillery shells on a small South Korean island, killing four people. But the South's taste for vengeance tends to fade quickly.

After international investigators confirmed that a North Korean torpedo sank the *Cheonan*, voters in the South refused to rally around President Lee, who had said the North Korean government should "pay a price." There was no South Korean version of the "9/11" effect that propelled the United States into wars in Afghanistan and Iraq. Instead, Lee's party was routed in a midterm election that showed that South Koreans were more interested in preserving peace and protecting living standards than in teaching the North a lesson.

"There is no winner if war breaks out, hot or cold," Lim Seung-youl,

27, a Seoul clothing distributor, told me. "Our nation is richer and smarter than North Korea. We have to use reason over confrontation."

South Koreans have spent decades refining what reason means in response to a next-door dictatorship that has moved about eighty percent of its total military firepower to within sixty miles of the Demilitarized Zone, the heavily guarded border strip that separates the two Koreas, and has repeatedly threatened to turn Seoul (located just thirty-five miles from the border) into a "sea of fire." Bloody surprise attacks from the North have a way of recurring every ten to fifteen years, from the 1968 raid by a hit squad that tried to assassinate a South Korean president, to the 1987 bombing of a Korean Air passenger jet and the failed 1996 submarine infiltration by special forces commandos, to the 2010 sinking of the warship and the shelling of the island.

The attacks have killed hundreds of South Koreans, but they have yet to provoke the electorate into demanding that their government launch a major counterattack. Nor have they stopped the average South Korean from getting richer, better educated, and better housed in what has become the fourth largest economy in Asia, the eleventh largest in the world.

South Koreans have paid close attention to the price tag of German unification. The proportional burden on South Korea, some studies have found, would be two and a half times greater than on West Germany after it absorbed the former East Germany. The studies found that it could cost more than two trillion dollars over thirty years, raise taxes for six decades, and require that ten percent of the South's gross domestic product be spent in the North for the foreseeable future.

South Koreans want reunification with the North, but they do not want it right away. Many do not want it during their lifetimes—largely because the cost would be unacceptably high.

Shin and many other North Korean defectors complain, with considerable justification, that South Koreans view them as ill-educated, ill-spoken, and badly dressed bumpkins whose mess of a country is more trouble than it is worth.

There is ample evidence that South Korean society makes it hard for defectors to fit in. The unemployment rate of North Koreans in the South is four times the national average; the suicide rate for defectors is more than two and a half times as high as the rate for South Koreans.

But South Koreans themselves struggle mightily to fit into their own success-obsessed, status-conscious, and education-crazed culture. Shin was attempting to find his way in a society that is singularly overworked, insecure, and stressed out. South Koreans work more, sleep less, and kill themselves at a higher rate than citizens of any other developed country, according to the Organization for Economic Cooperation and Development (OECD), a group that supports sustainable economic growth in thirty-four wealthy countries.

They also view each other with a witheringly critical eye. Self-worth tends to be narrowly defined by admission to a few highly selective universities and prestigious, high-paying jobs at conglomerates like Samsung, Hyundai, and LG.

"This society is unforgiving, relentless, and the competition is constant," Andrew Eungi Kim, a sociology professor at Korea University, one of the country's most elite schools, told me. "If young people do not obtain the right credentials—they call it the 'right spec'—they become very pessimistic. They believe they cannot get started in life. The pressure to do well in school begins to build at grade four, believe it or not, and it becomes everything to students by grade seven."

The pursuit of the "right spec" has supercharged spending on schooling. Among wealthy countries, South Korea ranks first in per capita spending on private education, which includes home tutors, cram sessions, and English-language courses at home and abroad. Four out of five students from elementary age to high school attend after-school cram courses. About six percent of the country's gross domestic product is spent on education, more than double the percentage of comparable spending in the United States, Japan, or Britain.

South Korea's obsession with achievement has paid astonishing dividends. International economists often describe South Korea as the single most impressive example of what free markets, democratic government, and elbow grease can do to transform a small agrarian backwater into a global powerhouse.

But the human cost of sudden affluence has also been astonishing.

Although the suicide rate in most other wealthy countries peaked in the early 1980s, it continues to climb in South Korea, doubling since 2000. The suicide rate in 2008 was two and half times higher than in the United States and significantly higher than in nearby Japan, where suicide is deeply embedded in the culture. It seems to have spread as a kind of infectious disease exacerbated by the strains of ambition, affluence, family disintegration, and loneliness.

"We are unwilling to seek help for depression. We are very afraid of being seen as crazy," Ha Kyooseob, a psychiatrist at Seoul National University College of Medicine and head of the Korean Association for Suicide Prevention, told me. "This is the dark aspect of our rapid development."

Although the stresses of affluence go a long way toward explaining South Korea's indifference to defectors like Shin, there is another important factor: a schism in public opinion about how to manage the risks of living next to North Korea.

Depending on which way the political winds are blowing, the public and the government in Seoul swing between blinkered conciliation and careful confrontation.

After coming into office in 2008, President Lee and his ruling party stiffened the government's attitude toward North Korea, cutting nearly all aid and applying conditions for cooperation on progress in nuclear disarmament and human rights. The policy has led to several jittery years of missile launches, frozen economic deals, border shootings, and periodic threats from the North of "total war."

Before Lee, South Korea took almost exactly the opposite approach. As part of its Sunshine Policy, presidents Kim Dae-jung and Roh Moo-hyun attended summits with Kim Jong Il in Pyongyang, approved massive shipments of food and fertilizer, and agreed to generous economic deals. The policy all but ignored the existence of the labor camps and made no attempt to monitor who in North Korea benefited from the aid. But it won Kim Dae-jung the Nobel Peace Prize.

The South's schizophrenia over how to deal with the North is occasionally acted out in a kind of Kabuki theater on the border between the two Koreas. There, defectors launch balloons bound for their homeland with messages intended to offend Kim Jong Il. The leaflets describe him as a drinker of pricey imported wine, a seducer of other men's wives, a murderer, a slaveholder, and "the devil."

I attended one of these balloon launches and watched police from Lee's government struggle to protect a North Korean defector named Park Sang Hak from angry unionists and university intellectuals, who insisted that nonthreatening engagement with Kim's government was the only permissible policy.

Before it was over, Park kicked one of the counterprotesters squarely in the head—a blow that sounded like a bat whacking a baseball. He spat on several others. He pulled a tear-gas revolver from his jacket and fired it into the air before police grabbed it. He failed to stop his opponents from ripping apart most of the bags containing anti-North Korean leaflets.

In the end, Park's group managed to launch just one of its ten balloons and tens of thousands of leaflets were spilled onto the ground.

Shin and I met for the first time on the day after that balloon debacle. He had not attended. Street confrontation was not his style. He had been watching old films of the Allied liberation of Nazi concentration camps, which included scenes of bulldozers unearthing corpses that Adolf Hitler's collapsing Third Reich had tried to hide.

"It is just a matter of time," Shin told me, before North Korea decides to destroy the camps. "I hope that the United States, through pressure and persuasion, can convince [the North Korean government] not to murder all those people in the camps."

Shin had not figured out how to pay his bills, make a living, or find a girlfriend in South Korea. But he had decided what he wanted to do with the rest of his life: he would be a human rights activist and raise international awareness about the existence of the labor camps.

To that end, he intended to leave South Korea and move to the United States. He had accepted an offer from Liberty in North Korea, the nonprofit that sponsored his first American trip. He was moving to Southern California.

CHAPTER 23

U.S.A.

On a cool late-summer evening in an oceanside suburb of Los Angeles, Shin stood in front of a small audience of Korean American teenagers. Dressed in a red T-shirt, jeans, and sandals, he looked relaxed and smiled sweetly at the attentive kids seated in stackable chairs. He was the featured speaker at the Torrance First Presbyterian Church. His topic, as always in public appearances, was life in Camp 14.

For more than a year, his sponsors at LiNK had been sending him to this kind of event and nagging him to prepare appropriate remarks. They wanted him to deliver a crisply organized, emotionally powerful speech, preferably in English, that would use his unique story to shake up American audiences, motivate volunteers, and perhaps raise money for the cause of North Korean human rights. As one of LiNK's executives told me, "Shin could be an incredible asset for us and this movement. 'You could be the face of North Korea,' we tell him."

Shin was not so sure.

On that night in Torrance, he had not prepared anything. After he was introduced by a LiNK staffer, he said hello to the students in Korean and asked, through a translator, if they had any questions.

When a girl in the audience asked him to explain how he escaped, he looked pained.

"This is really private and sensitive," he said. "I try to avoid talking about it as much as I can."

Reluctantly, he told a story about his escape that was short, sketchy, sanitized—and largely incomprehensible to someone who was not steeped in the details of his life.

"My story can be very heartbreaking," he said, wrapping up the session after about fifteen minutes. "I don't want you to be depressed."

He had bored and baffled his audience. One boy—clearly confused about who Shin was and what he had done in North Korea—asked a final question. What had it been like to serve in the North Korean military? Shin corrected the boy, saying he had not served in the Korean People's Army. "I was not worthy," he said.

After watching his appearance in the church, I pressed Shin to explain what was going on: Why do you want to be a human rights witness when it seems so difficult for you to talk in public about what happened in the camp? Why do you leave out the parts of your story that could rile up an audience?

"The things I went through were mine alone," he replied, not looking me in the eye. "I believe most people will find it nearly impossible to know what I am talking about."

Nightmares—images of his mother's hanging—continued to haunt his sleep. His screams woke up roommates in the group house he shared in Torrance with LiNK volunteers. He refused free counseling from Los Angeles–based, Korean-speaking psychotherapists. He declined to enroll in courses that could give him a high school equivalency degree. He refused to consider college.

Several times during our long weeks of interviews, he mentioned a "dead space" inside him, which he said made it difficult for him to feel much of anything. Sometimes he pretended to be happy, he said, to see how other people reacted to him. Often he did not make any effort.

Shin's adjustment to life in the United States had not been easy.

Shortly after arriving in California in the spring of 2009, Shin began having severe and recurring headaches. His colleagues at LiNK worried that he was suffering from post-traumatic stress disorder. It turned out the headaches were a symptom of runaway tooth decay. A dentist performed root canal surgery. The headaches went away.

That instant cure was the exception.

There is—there will be—no quick, easy way for Shin to adapt to life outside the fence, whether in the United States or in South Korea. His friends told me as much, and so did he.

"Shin is still a prisoner," said Andy Kim, a young Korean American who helped run LiNK and who, for a time, was Shin's closest confidant. "He cannot enjoy his life when there are people suffering in the camps. He sees happiness as selfishness."

Andy and Shin are about the same age and they often ate lunch together at Los Chilaquiles, a cheap Mexican joint in a strip mall not far from LiNK's office in a Torrance industrial park. Shin was passionate about food and did his best talking in Korean and Mexican restaurants. For several months, Andy met Shin once a week for an hour to discuss how his life was shaping up in the United States.

There were a number of good things going on. Shin had become chatty and playful in the office. He stunned Andy and others at LiNK by popping into their offices and telling them that he "loved" them. But he often did not respond well to advice from these same people, and had trouble distinguishing between constructive criticism and personal betrayal. Shin made little progress in learning how to manage money, sometimes spending more than he could afford on dinners and airline tickets for friends. In tearful conversations with Andy he would describe himself as "worthless garbage."

"Sometimes Shin sees himself through the eyes of his new self, and sometimes he sees himself through the eyes of the guards in the camp," said Andy. "He is kind of here and kind of there."

When I asked Shin if this was true, he nodded yes.

"I am evolving from being an animal," he said. "But it is going very, very slowly. Sometime I try to cry and laugh like other people, just to see if it feels like anything. Yet tears don't come. Laughter doesn't come."

His behavior was consistent with a pattern that researchers have found among concentration camp survivors the world over. They often move through life with what Harvard psychiatrist Judith Lewis Herman calls a "contaminated identity."

"They suffer not only from a classic post-traumatic syndrome but also from profound alterations in their relations with God, with other people, and with themselves," Herman wrote in her book, *Trauma and Recovery*, an examination of the psychological consequences of political terror. Most survivors are "preoccupied with shame, self-loathing, and a sense of failure."[1]

Soon after Shin arrived in California, Kyung Soon Chung, a pastor's wife born in Seoul, began cooking for him, mothering him, and monitoring his adjustment to American life. When he first showed up at her home for dinner, she ran to him and tried to give him a hug. He would not have it. He felt uncomfortable being touched.

But he kept coming to dinner, in part because he loved Kyung's cooking. He also had become friends with Kyung's twenty-something children: Eunice, a human rights activist he had met in Seoul, and her younger brother, David, a recent Yale graduate also interested in human rights. The family, which has befriended a number of North Korean immigrants, lives in Riverside, a city sixty miles east of Torrance. Kyung and her husband, Jung Kun Kim, head a small Christian ministry called the Ivy Global Mission.

Shin discovered a Korean family that was open, welcoming, and loving. He was envious and a bit overwhelmed by the intensity with which they cared for one another—and for him. For nearly two years, he spent every other Saturday evening at Kyung's dinner table. He slept over in a guest room and attended church with the family on Sunday.

Kyung, who doesn't speak much English, began calling Shin her eldest son. He tolerated—and then returned—her hugs. He learned that she loved frozen yogurt, and before coming to dinner he would stop at a supermarket and buy her some. She teased him, saying, "When are you going to bring me a daughter-in-law?" He flattered her, telling her that she was losing weight and looking younger. They talked for hours, just the two of them.

"Why are you so nice to me?" Shin once asked her, his mood darkening. "Don't you know what I have done?"

He told Kyung that he "disgusts" himself, that he cannot escape dreams of his mother's death, that he cannot forgive himself for leaving his father behind in the camp, and that he hates himself for crawling over Park's body. He said, too, that he was ashamed for stealing rice and clothing from poor North Koreans during his flight out of the country.

There will be no end to Shin's guilt, Kyung believes. But she often told him he had a powerful conscience and a good heart. She also said he had an advantage over other North Koreans: he had not been contaminated by propaganda or the cult of personality that surrounds the Kim dynasty.

"With Shin, there is a certain purity," she said. "He has never been brainwashed."

Her children saw striking changes in Shin's confidence and social skills after a couple of years in California: he was less shy, quicker to smile, and became something of a hugger. Before and after some of my interviews with him in California, he hugged me too.

"He used to be embarrassed meeting my church friends," said Eunice. "Now he knows how to make jokes. He laughs out loud."

David agreed. "Shin shows real empathy for others. This thing called love—he may have quite a lot of love in there."

Shin's self-assessment was less sanguine.

"Because I am surrounded by good people, I try to do what good people do," he told me. "But it is very difficult. It does not flow from me naturally."

In California, Shin began giving God all the credit for his escape from Camp 14 and for his good fortune in finding a way out of North Korea and China. His emerging Christian faith, though, did not square with the time line of his life. He did not hear about God until it was too late for his mother, his brother, and Park. He doubted too that God had protected his father from the vengeance of guards.

Similarly, guilt had not been an issue for Shin inside Camp 14. As an adolescent, he was furious with his mother for beating him, for risking escape, for causing his torture. He did not grieve when she was hanged. But as an adult survivor, as his emotional distance from the camp increases, his fury has given way to guilt and self-loathing. "These are emotions that slowly started to come out from within me," he said. Having seen firsthand how loving families behave, he cannot bear the memory of the kind of son he once was.

Shin had come to Torrance with the understanding that he would help LiNK by working with its volunteers and speaking at its events. In return, LiNK provided him with housing and a living stipend, but no salary. With LiNK's help, he obtained a ten-year multiple-entry visa that allowed him to stay in the United States for up to six months at a time.

U.S. immigration law grants special consideration to North Korean refugees, and Shin's unique status as a born and bred victim of a political prison camp gave him an excellent chance of obtaining permanent residency in the United States. But he did not apply for a green card. He could not decide where he wanted to live.

Committing to anything was difficult. He enrolled in an English-language course in Torrance, but dropped out after three months. He spent most of his time in LiNK's office, where he read North Korean news on the Web and chatted with Korean-speaking staff. He was sometimes content to sweep floors, sort boxes, and carry furniture. He told Hannah Song, the executive director, that he should be treated no differently than any other staff member. But he also pouted about work assignments and succumbed to fits of anger. Every six months his work was interrupted when he traveled back to South Korea for several weeks at a time.

LiNK pushes the North Koreans it helps bring to the United States to make a "life plan" soon after they arrive. It is a list of practical, achievable goals that can help a newcomer build a stable, productive life; it usually includes English fluency, job training, counseling, and lessons in money management.

Shin refused to make a life plan, and Song said she and others at LiNK allowed him to get away with it.

"His story is so powerful," said Song. "He felt entitled to be an exception, and we enabled him. He just floated around Torrance. He feels a need to make sense of why he survived that camp. I don't think he has figured it out yet."

Outside of the Korean Peninsula, there's no place easier than greater Los Angeles for a Korean to float around without learning another language. More than three hundred thousand Korean Americans have settled in and around the city.

In Torrance and adjacent towns, Shin could eat, shop, work, and worship in Korean. He learned enough English to order burgers and Mexican food and to talk about baseball and the weather with his housemates.

He slept on a bunk bed in the four-bedroom ranch-style house provided by LiNK, where up to sixteen college-age volunteers and interns came and went. In the kitchen, on the day I visited, the dishwasher displayed a sign that said: "Please don't open. I am broken and I smell bad." The furniture was worn, the carpet faded, and the wide front porch was littered with sneakers, sandals, and flip-flops. Shin shared a cramped bedroom with three LiNK volunteers.

The quasi-chaotic, dormlike camaraderie suited him. Although his American-born housemates were sometimes noisy, spoke little Korean, and never stayed around very long, he preferred their energetic transience to living alone. It was a lingering effect of the life he had known in Camp 14. He slept better and enjoyed food more when surrounded by people, even if they were strangers. When he struggled to fall asleep in the group house or when nightmares woke him up, he crawled out of his bunk and slept as he had in the camp—on a bare floor with a blanket.

Shin bicycled to work. It was an easy twenty-minute commute through Torrance, a sun-soaked, industrial-suburban, multicultural mishmash of a place. Located nineteen miles southwest of downtown Los Angeles, it has a fine stretch of beach on Santa Monica Bay, where Shin sometimes went for walks. The wide avenues of Torrance were drawn up a century ago by Frederick Law Olmsted Jr., who helped design the Mall in Washington. The Mediterranean Revival facade of Torrance High School was the backdrop for TV's *Beverly Hills, 90210* and *Buffy the Vampire Slayer*. Torrance also has an ExxonMobil refinery that churns out much of Southern California's gasoline. Before living in the group house, Shin spent much of his first year in Torrance in an aging, overcrowded, three-bedroom garden apartment that LiNK rented near a vast oil storage depot called the ConocoPhillips/Torrance Tank Farm.

LiNK moved to Torrance from Washington, D.C., to find cheaper rent and to focus on building a grassroots movement. It viewed Southern California as a better place to recruit and house the young volunteers it calls "Nomads." They are trained in Torrance to travel across the United States, give presentations, and raise awareness about human rights abuses in North Korea.

At the end of Shin's second summer in California, one of those newly arrived Nomads-in-training was Harim Lee, a slim and strikingly attractive young woman who was born in Seoul and moved to the United States with her family when she was four.

She attended high school in the suburbs of Seattle and was a second-year student studying sociology at the University of Washington when she first saw Shin in a YouTube video. He was speaking in an auditorium in Mountain View, California, answering questions about his life from people who worked at Google. She also found the *Washington Post* story I wrote about Shin, which quoted him saying he would like to have a girlfriend, but didn't know how to find one.

Harim, who is bilingual, had traveled back to South Korea to work briefly as a translator for an NGO, or nongovernmental organization, that focused on North Korea. After her third year in college, she decided to leave school and get involved full time in the North Korean issue. She learned about LiNK's Nomad program on the Web. She did not realize that Shin was living in Torrance until two weeks before she flew from Seattle to start at LiNK. On the flight to Los Angeles, she could not stop thinking about Shin. She regarded him as a celebrity and prayed on the plane that they would become close. In Torrance, she soon spotted him cruising into LiNK's office on his bicycle and made it her business to find a time and a place where they could talk. They liked each other immediately. He was twenty-seven; she was twenty-two.

LiNK has a strict no-dating rule between North Korean refugees and interns, many of whom are college age and far from their parents. The rule is intended to protect both the interns and the refugees, and ease the management challenges of the Nomad program.

Shin and Harim ignored the rule. When they were warned to stop seeing each other until she finished her internship, both became angry. Harim threatened to quit. "We made a big deal to show that we felt the rule was wrong," she told me.

Shin viewed the warning as a personal insult. He complained of a double standard that made him a second-class person, and noted that his confidant Andy Kim was dating an intern. "It is because they thought so little of me," Shin told me. "They thought they could rule my private life."

After a trip to South Korea and several months of brooding, Shin quit LiNK. His relationship with Harim was not the only reason behind the break. Hannah Song was frustrated that Shin sometimes avoided responsibility, expected special treatment, and made little effort to learn English, which limited his usefulness as a spokesman in the United States. There was also miscommunication about housing. As Shin heard it, LiNK would no longer provide him with a place to live. Song said she had told Shin that at some point he would have to find a place of his own.

The strain was probably inevitable. It certainly was not unusual. In South Korea, North Korean defectors routinely quit their jobs, claiming they have been singled out for persecution. At Hanawon, the reset-tlement center in South Korea, job counselors say that workplace paranoia, stormy resignations, and lingering feelings of betrayal are chronic problems as North Koreans adjust to new lives. Many of them never land on their feet.

In the United States, the pattern is similar. Cliff Lee, a Korean-born American who lives in Alexandria, Virginia, has provided housing to several North Koreans in recent years and seen a pattern in their adjustment troubles: "They know that everything they were told in North Korea was a lie, and they have a very tough time in America believing anything that an organization says."

Song was heartbroken by Shin's decision to quit. She blamed her-self for not demanding, when he first arrived in California, that he take responsibility for himself. Her main worry, she said, is not knowing what Shin is planning to do for the rest of his life.

EPILOGUE
NO ESCAPE

I n February 2011, days after his break with LiNK, Shin flew up the West Coast to Washington State. He moved in with Harim and her parents in Sammamish, a Seattle suburb in the western foothills of the Cascade Mountains.

His sudden relocation surprised me. I was also worried, like his friends in Los Angeles, that he was being impulsive and burning bridges without good reason. But his move certainly simplified the logistics of spending time with him. I happen to be from the state of Washington. After leaving Tokyo and the *Washington Post*, I had moved back to Seattle to work on this book. When Shin telephoned me at home and told me in broken English that he had become my neighbor, I invited him over for tea.

Our work together was nearly done, and Shin had kept his word. He had allowed me to move around in the darkest corners of his past. But I needed a bit more: a better sense of what he wanted in the future. As he sat with Harim on the couch in my living room, I asked if I could visit their home. I wanted to meet Harim's parents.

Shin and Harim were too polite to say no. Instead, they said the house was too messy. They would have to check on a good time. They would get back to me. Without saying so, they made it clear that they would prefer that my long interrogation come to an end—and soon.

He and Harim had formed a two-person NGO called North Korea Freedom Plexus. To fund it, they hoped to raise money from donations, and he intended to give a lot of speeches. Their ambitious mission was to open asylum shelters for defectors who crossed into China and to smuggle antiregime pamphlets into North Korea. To that end, Shin said he had twice traveled to border areas inside China and planned to do so again. When I asked if he was afraid of being abducted or arrested in China, where North Korean agents are known to hunt down and kidnap defectors, he said he has the protection of a South Korean passport and that he is always careful. But this was not an answer that satisfied friends who warned him to stay out of China.

Lowell and Linda Dye—the Columbus couple who read my first story about Shin in 2008 and helped pay for his travel to the United States—were disappointed and worried when they heard that he had quit LiNK and moved to Seattle. The Dyes and the Kim family in Riverside, California, have told Shin that creating a new NGO is a risky idea and that he would be more effective if he continued to work with a well-established and well-funded organization.

Shin has become close to the Dyes. He calls them his "parents" and takes their concerns seriously. After he moved to Seattle, he accepted an invitation to travel to Columbus and stay with them for a couple of weeks, while Harim stayed home in Seattle.

The Dyes wanted to help Shin make a plan for managing his future. Lowell, a management consultant, believes he needs an agent, a money manager, and a lawyer. But in Columbus, he and Shin did not have a serious talk, in part because Shin kept Seattle hours, sleeping in until late morning and staying up at night to talk to Harim on Skype.

"He told us he really loves Harim," Lowell said. "That is the way he is going. She makes him happy."

When Shin returned to Seattle, I met again with him and Harim. Their house was still too messy, they said, for me to visit, so we had coffee at Starbucks. When I asked how their relationship was going, Harim blushed, smiled, and looked lovingly at Shin.

Shin did not smile.

He did not want to talk about it.

I persisted, reminding him that he had often told me he did not consider himself capable of love, certainly not of marriage. Had he changed his mind?

"We have to work before anything else," he said. "But after work is done there is hope for progress."

The relationship did not work out. Six months after he moved in with Harim, Shin called me to say that they were splitting up. He did not want to talk about why. Shin flew the next day to Ohio to live with the Dye family. He was not certain where he would go from there, perhaps back to South Korea.

While Shin was still in the Seattle area, he invited me to a Korean American Pentecostal church in the city's northern suburbs. He was giving a speech and seemed especially eager that I come and listen. When I showed up at the church a few minutes early on a cold and rainy Sunday evening, he was waiting for me. He shook my hand with both of his, looked me in the eye, and told me to sit in a pew near the front. He was dressed more formally than I could remember seeing him: a gray business suit, a blue dress shirt open at the collar, polished black loafers. The church was full.

After a hymn and a prayer from the pastor, Shin strode to the front of the church and took command of the evening. Without notes, without a hint of nerves, he spoke for a solid hour. He began by goading his audience of Korean immigrants and their American-raised adult children, asserting that Kim Jong Il was worse than Hitler. While Hitler attacked his enemies, Shin said Kim worked his own people to death in places like Camp 14.

Having grabbed the congregation's attention, Shin then introduced himself as a predator who had been bred in the camp to inform on family and friends—and to feel no remorse. "The only thing I thought was that I had to prey on others for my survival," he said.

In the camp, when his teacher beat a six-year-old classmate to death for having five grains of corn in her pocket, Shin confessed to the congregation that he "didn't think much about it."

"I did not know about sympathy or sadness," he said. "They educated us from birth so that we were not capable of normal human emotions. Now that I am out, I am learning to be emotional. I have learned to cry. I feel like I am becoming human."

But Shin made it clear that he still had a long way to go. "I escaped physically," he said. "I haven't escaped psychologically."

Near the end of his speech, Shin described how he had crawled over Park's smoldering body. His motives in fleeing Camp 14, he said, were not noble. He did not thirst for freedom or political rights. He was merely hungry for meat.

Shin's speech astonished me. Compared to the diffident, incoherent speaker I had seen six months earlier in Southern California, he was unrecognizable. He had harnessed his self-loathing and used it to indict the state that had poisoned his heart and killed his family.

His confessional, I later learned, was the calculated result of hard work. Shin had noticed that his meandering question-and-answer sessions were putting people to sleep. So he decided to act on advice he had been resisting for years: he outlined his speech, tailored it to his audience, and memorized what he wanted to say. In a room by himself, he polished his delivery.

Preparation paid off. That evening, his listeners squirmed in their pews, their faces showing discomfort, disgust, anger, and shock. Some faces were stained with tears. When Shin was finished, when he told the congregation that one man, if he refuses to be silenced, could help free the tens of thousands who remain in North Korea's labor camps, the church exploded in applause.

In that speech, if not yet in his life, Shin had seized control of his past.

APPENDIX

THE TEN LAWS OF CAMP 14

(Shin was required in the camp's school to memorize these rules, and he was often ordered by guards to recite them.)

1. **Do not try to escape.**

   Anyone caught escaping will be shot immediately.

   Any witness to an attempted escape who fails to report it will be shot immediately.

   Any witness to an attempted escape must promptly notify a guard.

   Groups of two or more are prohibited from assembling to devise a plot or to attempt to escape.

2. **No more than two prisoners can meet together.**

   Anyone who fails to secure permission from a guard for a meeting of more than two prisoners will be shot immediately.

   Those who trespass into the guards' village or who damage public property will be shot immediately.

   No gathering may exceed the number of prisoners allowed by the guard in charge.

Outside work, no group of prisoners may gather without permission.

At night, three or more prisoners may not travel together without permission from the guard in charge.

3. Do not steal.

Anyone found stealing or in possession of arms will be shot immediately.

Anyone who does not report or who aids a person who has stolen or possesses arms will be shot immediately.

Anyone who steals or conceals any foodstuffs will be shot immediately.

Anyone who deliberately damages any materials used in the camp will be shot immediately.

4. Guards must be obeyed unconditionally.

Anyone who harbors ill will toward or physically assaults a guard will be shot immediately.

Anyone who fails to demonstrate total compliance with a guard's instructions will be shot immediately.

There must be no backtalk or complaints to a guard.

When meeting a guard, one must bow deferentially.

5. Anyone who sees a fugitive or suspicious figure must promptly report him.

Anyone who provides cover for or protects a fugitive will be shot immediately.

Anyone who holds or hides a fugitive's possessions, conspires with him, or fails to report him will be shot immediately.

6. **Prisoners must watch one another and report any suspicious behavior immediately.**

   Each prisoner must observe others and remain vigilant.

   The speech and conduct of others must be observed closely. Should anything arouse suspicion, a guard must be notified immediately.

   Prisoners must faithfully attend meetings of ideological struggle, and they must censure others and themselves vehemently.

7. **Prisoners must more than fulfill the work assigned them each day.**

   Prisoners who neglect their work quota or fail to complete it will be considered to harbor discontent and will be shot immediately.

   Each prisoner must be solely responsible for his work quota.

   To fulfill one's work quota is to wash away sins, as well as to recompense the state for the forgiveness it has shown.

   The work quota as assigned by a guard may not be changed.

8. **Beyond the workplace, there must be no intermingling between the sexes for personal reasons.**

   Should sexual physical contact occur without prior approval, the perpetrators will be shot immediately.

   Beyond the workplace, there must be no conversing between the sexes without prior approval.

   One is prohibited from visiting bathrooms designated for members of the opposite sex without prior approval.

   Without special reason, members of opposite sexes may not go about holding hands or sleep alongside each other.

   Without prior approval, prisoners may not visit living quarters of the opposite sex.

9. Prisoners must genuinely repent of their errors.

Anyone who does not acknowledge his sins and instead denies them or carries a deviant opinion of them will be shot immediately.

One must reflect deeply upon the sins he has committed against his country and society and strive to wash himself of them.

Only after having acknowledged sins and reflected deeply upon them can a prisoner begin anew.

10. Prisoners who violate the laws and regulations of the camp will be shot immediately.

All prisoners must truly consider the guards as their teachers, and, abiding by the ten laws and regulations of the camp, yield themselves through toil and discipline to washing away their past errors.

ACKNOWLEDGMENTS

This book, of course, could not have been written without the courage, intelligence, and patience of Shin Dong-hyuk. For two years and on two continents, he took the time and endured the pain of telling his story in all its awful detail.

I also want to thank Lisa Colacurcio, a member of the board of the U.S. Committee for Human Rights in North Korea, who first told me about Shin. Kenneth Cukier, a correspondent at *The Economist*, told me that Shin's story needed a book in English and offered useful suggestions about how to write it.

Since I do not speak Korean, I depended on translators. I would like to thank Stella Kim and Jennifer Cho in Seoul. Also in Seoul, Yoonjung Seo helped with reporting, as did Brian Lee. In Tokyo, Akiko Yamamoto helped with reporting and logistics. In Southern California, David Kim was a masterful translator and friend to Shin and to me. He also gave me advice on the manuscript.

At Liberty in North Korea (LiNK) in Torrance, Hannah Song and Andy Kim helped me understand Shin's adjustment to the United States. In addition, Song spent many hours solving logistical problems for Shin and for me. In Seattle, Harim Lee was also helpful. In Columbus, Ohio, Lowell and Linda Dye, who have helped Shin and whom he regards as parents, offered perspective and advice.

For guidance in my attempt to understand what is going on inside North Korea, I thank Marcus Noland, deputy director and senior fellow at the Peterson Institute for International Economics in Washington. He gave generously of his time and expertise. His research on North Korea with Stephan Haggard was a key resource. Also, conversations with Kongdan Oh, a research staff member at the Institute for Defense Analyses in Alexandria, Virginia, helped me understand what I heard from Shin and from other North Koreans. The books she has written with her husband, Ralph Hassig, a North Korean scholar, were also invaluable. In Seoul, Andrei Lankov, who teaches North Korean studies at Kookmin University, was always willing to share his insight.

Two tireless bloggers, Joshua Stanton from One Free Korea and Curtis Melvin of North Korean Economy Watch, provided useful and constantly updated information and analysis about the North's economy, leadership, military, and politics. Also, Barbara Demick's fine book, *Nothing to Envy*, was a key to the thinking of ordinary North Koreans.

I especially want to thank the Seoul-based Database Center for North Korean Human Rights. It published Shin's Korean-language memoir and generously encouraged him to cooperate with me. Also, the Korean Bar Association's "White Paper on Human Rights in North Korea 2008" was a valuable resource.

David Hawk, author of "The Hidden Gulag: Exposing North Korea's Prison Camps" and perhaps the single most important individual in alerting outsiders to the existence and operation of the camps, shared his expertise and research. Suzanne Scholte, who has led campaigns around the world for human rights in North Korea, also has my thanks. In Seattle, Blaise Aguera y Arcas made shrewd narrative suggestions and Sam Howe Verhovek gave reporting advice.

My agent, Raphael Sagalyn, did a masterful job in making this book possible. At Viking, editor Kathryn Court embraced this project and offered advice that significantly improved the manuscript, as did Tara Singh, Kathryn's assistant.

David Hoffman, the *Washington Post* foreign editor who sent me to Asia, told me to dig into North Korea. When I hesitated, he insisted. When I struggled, he was encouraging. *Post* editors Doug Jehl and Kevin Sullivan were also demanding and supportive. Donald G. Graham, the chairman of the Washington Post Company, paid amazingly close attention to North Korea and always let me know when I managed to write anything interesting about it.

Finally, my wife, Jessica Kowal, played a major role in making this book. In addition to reading and editing it, she convinced me that telling Shin's story was the best possible thing I could do. My children, Lucinda and Arno, asked a lot of good questions about Shin's life. They could not comprehend the cruelty of North Korea, but recognized Shin as an amazing person. I feel the same way.

NOTES

NOTES

INTRODUCTION: NEVER HEARD THE WORD "LOVE"

1. Amnesty International, "Images Reveal Scale of North Korean Political Prison Camps," May 3, 2011, http://www.amnesty.org/en/news-and-updates/images-reveal-scale-north-korean-political-prison-camps-2011-05-03.

2. Kang Chol-hwan and Pierre Rigoulot, *The Aquariums of Pyongyang* (New York: Basic Books, 2001), 79.

3. These eyewitnesses, including Shin, have been interviewed by David Hawk, a researcher for the U.S. Committee on Human Rights in North Korea. Their stories and satellite photos of the camps can be found in Hawk's periodically updated report, "The Hidden Gulag: Exposing North Korea's Prison Camps," first published in 2003.

4. Korean Bar Association, "White Paper on Human Rights in North Korea 2008" (Seoul: Korea Institute for National Unification, 2008).

5. American television journalists Laura Ling and Euna Lee spent nearly five months in North Korean prisons after crossing illegally into the country in 2009. They were released after former president Bill Clinton flew to Pyongyang and had his picture taken with Kim Jong Il.

6. Hyun-sik Kim and Kwang-ju Son, *Documentary Kim Jong Il* (Seoul: Chonji Media, 1997), 202, as cited in Ralph Hassig and Kongdan Oh, *The Hidden People of North Korea* (Lanham, Md.: Rowman & Littlefield, 2009), 27.

CHAPTER ONE: THE BOY WHO ATE HIS MOTHER'S LUNCH

1. Author interview with Chun Jung-hee, head nurse at Hanawon resettlement center in South Korea. The government-funded center has measured and weighed North Korean defectors since 1999.

CHAPTER THREE: THE UPPER CRUST

1. Author interviews with defectors between 2007 and 2010. The system is also well described by Andrei Lankov in *North of the DMZ* (Jefferson, N.C.: McFarland & Company, 2007), 67–69; and by Hassig and Oh in *The Hidden People of North Korea*, 198–99.
2. Details on the lifestyle of Kim Jong Il are gathered in Hassig and Oh, 27–35. See also Google Earth photographs compiled by Curtis Melvin, on his blog, North Korean Economy Watch, http://www.nkeconwatch.com/2011/06/10/friday-fun-kim-jong-ils-train/.
3. Andrew Higgins, "Who Will Succeed Kim Jong Il," *Washington Post* (July 16, 2009), A1.

CHAPTER NINE: REACTIONARY SON OF A BITCH

1. Kang and Rigoulot, *The Aquariums of Pyongyang*, 100.
2. Kim Yong, *Long Road Home* (New York: Columbia University Press, 2009), 85.

CHAPTER TEN: WORKING MAN

1. Andrea Matles Savada, ed., *North Korea: A Country Study* (Washington, D.C.: GPO for the Library of Congress, 1993).
2. Yuk-Sa Li, ed., *Juche! The Speeches and Writings of Kim Il Sung* (New York: Grossman Publishers, 1972), 157. Quoted in the *Stanford Journal of East Asian Affairs* 1, no. 1 (Spring 2003), 105.

CHAPTER ELEVEN: NAPPING ON THE FARM

1. Stephan Haggard and Marcus Noland, *Famine in North Korea* (New York: Columbia University Press, 2007), 175.
2. Wonhyuk Lim, "North Korea's Economic Futures" (Washington, D.C., Brookings Institution, 2005).

CHAPTER THIRTEEN: DECIDING NOT TO SNITCH

1. Elmer Luchterhand, "Prisoner Behavior and Social System in the Nazi Camp," *International Journal of Psychiatry* 13 (1967), 245–64.
2. Eugene Weinstock, *Beyond the Last Path* (New York: Boni and Gaer, 1947), 74.
3. Ernest Schable, "A Tragedy Revealed: Heroines' Last Days," *Life* (August 18, 1958), 78–144. Cited by Shamai Davidson in "Human Reciprocity Among the Jewish Prisoners in the Nazi Concentration Camps," *The Nazi Concentration Camps* (Jerusalem: Yad Vashem, 1984), 555–72.
4. Terrence Des Pres, *The Survivor: An Anatomy of Life in the Death Camps* (New York: Oxford University Press, 1976), 142.

CHAPTER FOURTEEN: PREPARING TO RUN

1. Yong, *Long Road Home*, 106.
2. Park was excessively hopeful. The United Nations, which created a Special Rapporteur for North Korean human rights in 2004, has gained no traction in influencing the government in Pyongyang. Nor has it had much success in raising international awareness about the camps. North Korea adamantly refused to allow the U.N.'s human rights representative into the country and condemned his annual reports as plots to overthrow the government. The reports have been among the most consistently critical—and incisively written—analyses of the human rights crisis in the North. In 2009, when he finished his six-year term as rapporteur, Vitit Muntarbhorn said, "The exploitation of the ordinary people . . . has become the pernicious prerogative of the ruling elite." He added that "[t]he human rights situation in the country remains abysmal owing to the repressive nature of the power base: at once cloistered, controlled and callous."

CHAPTER SIXTEEN: STEALING

1. Yoonok Chang, Stephan Haggard, Marcus Noland, "Migration Experiences of North Korean Refugees: Survey Evidence from China" (Washington, D.C.: Peterson Institute, 2008), 1.

CHAPTER SEVENTEEN: RIDING NORTH

1. Lankov, *North of the DMZ*, 180–83.
2. See Daily NK, October 25, 2010, for a detailed description of the *servi-cha* system and another attempt by the government to try to shut it down. http://www.dailynk.com/english/read.php?cataId=nk01500&num=6941.
3. Andrew S. Natsios, *The Great North Korean Famine* (Washington, D.C.: United States Institute for Peace Press, 2001), 218.
4. Charles Robert Jenkins, *The Reluctant Communist* (Berkeley: University of California Press, 2008), 129.
5. Barbara Demick, *Nothing to Envy* (New York: Spiegel & Grau, 2009), 159–72.

CHAPTER EIGHTEEN: THE BORDER

1. Human Rights Watch, "Harsher Policies Against Border-Crossers" (March 2007).
2. Lankov, *North of the DMZ*, 183.
3. Author interview in Seoul with officials from Good Friends, a Buddhist nonprofit organization with informants based inside North Korea.

CHAPTER NINETEEN: CHINA

1. Chang et al., "Migration Experiences of North Korean Refugees," 9.
2. Demick, *Nothing to Envy*, 163.
3. *Rimjin-gang: News from Inside North Korea*, edited by Jiro Ishimaru (Osaka: AsiaPress International, 2010), 11–15.
4. United Nations International Covenant on Civil and Political Rights, Article 12 (2), http://www2.ohchr.org/english/law/ccpr.htm.

CHAPTER TWENTY: ASYLUM

1. Lee Gwang Baek, "Impact of Radio Broadcasts in North Korea," speech at International Conference on Human Rights, November 1, 2010, http://nknet.org/eng/board/jbbs_view.
2. Peter M. Beck, "North Korea's Radio Waves of Resistance," *Wall Street Journal* (April 16, 2010).